NEW PREACHING
FROM THE
NEW TESTAMENT

NEW PREACHING FROM THE NEW TESTAMENT

D. W. Cleverley Ford

MOWBRAYS
LONDON & OXFORD

© *A. R. Mowbray & Co Ltd* 1977

ISBN 0 264 66401 9

First published in 1977
by A. R. Mowbray & Co. Ltd
Saint Thomas House,
Becket Street, Oxford. OX1 1SJ

Text set in 12 13pt *Monotype Bembo by Cotswold Typesetting Ltd., Gloucester*
Printed in Great Britain by Lowe & Brydone Printers Limited, Thetford, Norfolk

CONTENTS

ACKNOWLEDGEMENTS

Once again I wish to acknowledge my appreciation of the encouragement given me by Richard Mulkern, one of the Directors of the Publishing Department of Messrs A. R. Mowbray and Co., Ltd. Also to thank those who have invited me to preach in their pulpits, and thus produce some of the material contained in this book. A preacher without a pulpit of his own, as is my case, is dependent on the kindness of other preachers if he is to preach at all. And thirdly, I express my indebtedness to Mrs J. Hodgson who has prepared so many of my manuscripts for publication. Lastly may I thank Messrs Collins for permission to quote from *The Door Wherein I Went* by Lord Hailsham, and also Don Cupitt, Dean of Emmanuel College, Cambridge for permission to quote from an article of his in 'the Listener' in 1976.

Lambeth Palace 1977   *D. W. Cleverley Ford*

INTRODUCTION

When the title *New Preaching from the New Testament* was first suggested to me as a sequel to my *New Preaching from the Old Testament*, I was not attracted. I could not imagine myself producing new material from what is after all a small book, the New Testament, and which has been worked over for well nigh two thousand years by a multitude of preachers. What had I to say that could possibly be new?

Let it be supposed, however, for one rash moment, that I could produce completely new material, would it be Christian preaching? Is not Christian preaching committed to the task of exposing and applying certain historical events from which it is impossible to get away? In other words, it has to handle a tradition, it has to draw upon what the New Testament itself calls 'a deposit'. The only sense then in which new preaching from the New Testament can be new is that it is fresh preaching.

Yet there is a sense in which every sermon is new because every preacher is new. There are no copies or repeats of preachers, because there are no copies or repeats of persons. Every individual is different from every other individual. And so there cannot be two sermons exactly alike, every sermon must be new, because every preacher is new.

Every sermon must also be new because the occasion when it is preached is new. Even if a sermon is preached one Sunday and repreached verbatim the following Sunday it will not be the same sermon, it will be a new sermon. Why? Because the circumstances in which it is preached the second time are not the same. To take an extreme case; if, during the intervening week the river that winds through the town overflows its bank with much inconvenience and some loss of life to the inhabitants, last week's acceptable sermon on the love of God, if preached again, will sound very different in this week's desperate situation, it may even be resented.

And not only do the circumstances of the listening congregation change, so also does the preacher himself. He is not exactly the same preacher as he was last week, or will be next week. One week his faith may be supporting him joyously, but next week the clouds may have all but totally eclipsed his sun.

Let me repeat, therefore. Readers who take up this book expecting completely new themes will be disappointed. I make no apology, however, for if it were a book of this nature it would be a failure for the purpose I had in mind in writing it, which is to assist my fellow ordinary preachers in their ordinary pulpit ministries to make new sermons. Novel, idiosyncratic material would be useless because unable to be reshaped and adapted. But in as much as what is provided in the following pages has been used in situations as diverse as a village church, a cathedral, a Royal Chapel, and a girls' public school assembly, it is hoped that it can be worked over for use in as many other different places where Christian people assemble to worship the God and Father made known to us in the new man Jesus Christ our Lord, and the issue will indeed be 'new preaching from the New Testament'.

1 THE NEW PREACHING

2 Corinthians 5.17 (NEB) *'When anyone is united to Christ, there is a new world; the old order has gone, and a new order has already begun'*

If you are looking for excellence of literary style you need not trouble yourself with the New Testament, it is all there in the Old. If you are searching for wise maxims by which to rule your everyday life, where will you find better than in the Book of Proverbs in the Old Testament. If you are depressed, down-in-spirit, sensing nothing so much as the futility of human existence—and who is there who does not know the meaning of this, sometimes soaked in doubt?—where in the New Testament can you light on any passage to equal what is written in Ecclesiastes in the Old Testament? And to move nearer the bone, the love of God, the forgiveness of God, the long-suffering of God, the judgement of God, yes, and justice, mercy and humility, it is all there in the Old Testament, set out in places in the most moving of moving stories that have captivated the imagination of generations inscribing these values in hearts, minds and wills indelibly. There is nothing in the New Testament that cannot be found in the Old Testament, not omitting the teaching of Jesus, nothing, let it be emphasised, nothing except one thing, the Person of Jesus Christ himself. He is the one utterly new thing in the New Testament. He is what makes it new, he is what makes everything else new, and why there is new preaching from the New Testament.

1 *The Person of Christ*

What do we know about Jesus Christ? Very little indeed if what we insist on being given is documentary evidence apart from the gospels (which are Church writings), though there are brief allusions to him in the Latin writers Tacitus and Suetonius. But what do we know about him from the New

Testament itself? To some this will sound a silly question fit only for a silly answer, but scholars are not wanting who tell us that the gospels provide us not with what Jesus actually was in himself, but what the early Church believed about him. That is to say, even with the New Testament in our hands we still do not come within visible distance of Jesus. He remains beyond us, an unknown, inaccessible being. This is a disturbing assessment (not that it is novel, for it was being put about at least in 1913), but if it is true, then the one thing which gives the New Testament a right to uniqueness over against the Old, namely, Jesus Christ, is too shadowy to account for it.

But will this assessment hold? Are we as bereft of knowledge about Jesus as this theory suggests? Have we only interpretation but no basic history? Of course there is interpretation of Jesus in the New Testament. There is also theologizing, some of it rudimentary as in the book of the Acts of the Apostles, some of it profound, as in the Epistle to the Ephesians. What is more, there is interpretation of Jesus in the gospels themselves, notably the fourth, but also in the first three, the Synoptics. The gospels are not biographies of Jesus, they are proclamations, with Jesus as the object of the proclamations. And there can be little doubt that as regards the literary form of the gospels much is due to actual early Church preaching. *Am Anfang war die Kerygma* wrote Dibelius, and it is true. 'In the beginning was the preaching.' Yes, but what sparked off the preaching? What caused the theologizing? What was the something which existed, crying out for an interpretation? Every effect must have a cause. So we are driven to assert that if a Jesus did not exist, someone very like the pictures of him we are given in the gospels would have to be invented. Why? In order to account for the New Testament itself, and for the existence of the Christian Church. Without Jesus we should find ourselves in the absurd position of having to assert that the New Testament writers *about* Christ are more worthy of worship than the Christ about whom they wrote.

And someone complains that all this is tough going, difficult to follow. Perhaps it is. So let us ease it with an illustration. In

Emily Brontë's classical novel *Wuthering Heights* is a breath-taking description of a storm on the moors. As you read you feel you are there, so realistic is the writing. All the majesty, the fierceness and the danger force their way into your conscious-ness. But how came a woman to write all this? Even if we are ignorant of the background we shall have to agree that this cannot be the mere product of the imagination. Nor was it. At the age of six Emily Brontë lived through (and actually loved) a crashing storm on the moors near her home. It was this which lay behind the description as it occurs in *Wuthering Heights* she came one day to write.

Of this then we can be certain, something astonishing happened to produce the new preaching which produced the New Testament, and that something was Jesus Christ himself. And because no subsequent disclosure of God took place in any way comparable to that which was believed to have been given in Jesus, all memories in the early Church were ransacked to produce records as authentic as were possible of what he was and did and said. He was, he is, *the revelation*, therefore the need for him to be made known was paramount, and to assert that the early Church had no interest in such details of his life as were accessible is to misread the situation.

2 *The resurrection of Christ*

Jesus Christ then was the new thing which accounted for the new preaching and accounts for the New Testament. But what specifically about Jesus Christ? What was there about his life and ministry which wrenched round from their crippling despair the men and women who were captivated by his personality and saw him crucified? There is only one answer capable of standing the test of examination and that is his resurrection from the dead.

Maybe we have heard this so often we have ceased to be aware of the unlikelihood of his resurrection being invented. The descent of an angel to reveal God's purpose for mankind, yes, there is Old Testament precedent and even a hint in the gospel narratives themselves, but resurrection? No! Or some natural calamity such as an earthquake bringing home the presence of God in judgement upon a guilty people. There is a suggestion of this too in the gospels. Resurrection, however, the resurrection of a man within time is utterly new, so new as not to be conjectured. And as if this were not sufficiently novel, the gospels tell of resurrection *on the third day*.

In the *Times* on 17 April 1976, Daniel Jenkins, Minister of Regent Square United Reformed Church, London, wrote of the significance of the 'third day'. It was the rule of Eastern hospitality for a guest to remain with his host for three days. The first was a rest-day, the second a 'drest day' for ceremony and feasting, and the third was the day of departure. In the early Church also, one of the tests of authenticity of a travelling prophet was that he should have the good manners and sense to move on before the end of the third day. A similar distinction existed in relation to death itself. There was an old Jewish belief that the soul of a dead person hovered near the corpse for three days but that on the fourth, when decomposition began, it departed. To say that Jesus rose on the third day, therefore, would be taken to mean that he visited the realm of death but that death was unable to hold him as a permanent inhabitant. This is what Peter preached in his first sermon as recorded in Acts 2.24. It was new preaching.

3 *Union with Christ*

And so we are in a position to make three points. First, because of this resurrection of Jesus on the third day new preaching came into being. Secondly, what was proclaimed was Jesus as Lord, and thirdly, stories from his life were employed to illustrate it.

All preaching derived from the New Testament must have this quality of newness about it, or it is not in the apostolic succession of preaching. It must offer Christ, God's new man. It must offer him so as to evoke faith in him, which faith will turn out to be the means of uniting with Christ, and when that happens, such a difference is produced that it can only be described as 'a new world; the old order has gone, and a new order has already begun'.

Can we not find some parallel to this in a woman getting married? She enjoys her life—in a way. She is deeply interested in her work—in a way. She derives much from the companionship of her friends—in a way. But when the man whom she secretly admires asks her to marry him and she sets up her own home, somehow everything is different. She is the same person. She lives in the same locality. She may even continue with her old job, but for her there is 'a new world; the old order has gone, and a new order has already begun'.

So the transformation brought about in a life by union with Christ is not the mere product of pulpit rhetoric. On the contrary, it has witness borne to it by ten thousand times ten thousand people down through history, from Saul of Tarsus to Augustine, to Luther, to John Bunyan, to Cardinal Newman, to Pope John, to the latest convert in some charismatic meeting. And when these enter their new world of personal experience they make, and strive to make, a new world around them. This is how Christ is creative in the world today. A new order began with him in history and a new order comes into being with everyone and with every community, united to him. Such is the new preaching from the New Testament, or as St Paul wrote to the Corinthians, 'When any one is united to Christ, there is a new world; the old order has gone, and a new order has already begun.'

2 SAFEGUARDING THE SAVIOUR

John 1.14 (NEB) '*So the Word became flesh*'

There was published in 1976 a book which can scarcely be said to have received an enthusiastic welcome—if such an understatement will be pardoned. It is called *Christian Believing*, the work of the Church of England Doctrine Commission. The main criterion was that it failed to set out the content of what can be preached and believed in the modern world. Yet there are positive points in the book, not least in the 'Joint Report' section. For example, the Creeds are described as safeguards of the apostolic preaching. Professor Lampe writes, 'Those who drew them up and ratified them believed that by their means they were safeguarding the true interpretation of scriptures . . . setting out beyond all possibility of misunderstanding *the vital elements of the apostolic preaching.*'

But can we accept this? Can we accept it of *every statement* in the Apostles' Creed? Can we accept it of the phrase 'born of the Virgin Mary'? Do we really see this as safeguarding the apostolic preaching?

Imagine the Norfolk Broads for a moment, say, Hickling Broad in particular. For those unacquainted with them let it be added that they are shallow sheets of water, or lakes, set in a flat landscape, and Hickling Broad comprises some four hundred acres. Obviously they are almost ideal for sailing, not least because there is usually a sufficient supply of steady wind. But there is one hazard. Being shallow, there has to be marked out those parts of the Broad which are deep enough to take the keel or centre-board of sailing boats. So stout, tarred wooden piles have been driven into the bed of the Broad, projecting some six feet or more above the surface of the water. For safe sailing it is necessary to keep within the channel marked by the piles.

Can we see the statements of the Apostles' Creed in the light of this? Can we visualise them as stout wooden piles marking out the safe channel of Christian believing, and not only of Christian believing, but of the apostolic preaching? Notice how the piles allow freedom of movement on the Broad. No areas are positively fenced off. Boats may sail where they will, *but they do so at their own peril*, and no one is to be blamed except those sailing their craft if they find their keel embedded in the mud. So with statements of the Creed. No one is forced to abide by them but Christians are advised, if they do not wish to put their faith in jeopardy, not to stray too far away from the channel they indicate.

But what about the phrase, 'born of the Virgin Mary'? Is this pile really necessary? How can it be a safeguard? What danger is likely without it? This is a searching question for which not every one has the patience, and maybe that too is dangerous.

1 *Not anti-sex*

First, let it be said quite firmly that the statement concerning Jesus, that he was 'born of the Virgin Mary' is not there in order to safeguard Mary from anything to do with sex, because sex is an impure thing, if not an evil thing. It is true this view has been held by Christians. Some of the early Church Fathers taught that sex was one of the consequences of the Fall of Man into sin from his original state of goodness. This is not so. Sex is part of the created order, an order labelled in the book of Genesis as good. It has its continuance through sexual reproduction. Not that sex is free from *the possibility* of being sinful. On the contrary, it is one of those areas in human life where sinfulness can most easily gain a hold, and where the consequences can turn out to be most corrupt. Sex is not an incorruptible divine instinct, whatever pagan religion and so-called modern liberated men and women half believe. Neither is it intrinsically dirty. Nevertheless, because its essential dirtiness must be denied, this does not mean that sex must be, or even ought to be, paraded. There is a reticence about sex which is proper, its potential for good and evil is too great to be trivialised. We affirm then that the phrase, 'born of the Virgin Mary' is not in the Creed to keep sex away from Mary, the mother of Jesus, because it is essentially a dirty thing. This is the first point.

2 *Preaching not biography*

A second point to be noted, also negative, is that the phrase 'born of the Virgin Mary' is not in the Creed in order to safeguard every detail of the traditional Christmas story as received from the records in the gospels of St Matthew and St Luke. This is not to say that those accounts are without historical foundation. It is not even to say that Jesus' birth of a virgin mother is without historical foundation. What needs to be asserted is that what the gospels of St Matthew and St Luke provide is preaching, not introductory chapters in two biographies of Jesus. By means of stories about his infancy they proclaim Jesus and his significance 'for us men and for our salvation'. Let the point be made again. There is history in these narratives, there is also literary structuring, and there is exposition or homiletical teaching. To be technical for a moment, the birth narratives are composed of historico-literary-midrash, in fact they are similar in this respect to a sermon whose aim is not primarily to provide information about what happened, but to move the hearers to accept Jesus as Lord and Saviour.

3 *God has come*

So we ask for the *third time*—what does the phrase, 'born of the Virgin Mary' safeguard? And we answer—it safeguards Jesus as *The One from God*.

Let us pause at this point for a moment. Here is a man aged about thirty-two, working as an insurance agent in the City of London. He is married with two small children, and every day he travels to and fro on the Bakerloo underground train from his home in Pinner. He has had to take out a mortgage on his house, the repayment of which is a burden, and will be for years. To make matters worse, with redundancy striking at all forms of employment, he is not certain how secure is his job and the salary he earns. This anxiety is not something he dares to share with his wife, though at times he reckons she must guess. Anyway, she has trouble enough, one of the children is a spastic needing constant care. There is no opportunity for her to go out to work.

Here is the probing question. Of what value is it for this insurance agent to be informed that Jesus was born of the

Virgin Mary? Of what value more than to be provided with the facts about the childhood of Queen Nefertiti in the fourteenth century BC in Egypt? What bearing can it possibly have on his life, his mortgage, his problems and his fears for the future? Surely none, except possibly by way of diversion from his own real world!

What then is 'born of the Virgin Mary' safeguarding for this insurance agent, for some nurse in Wigan, a fitter in Wolverhampton, and a retired pensioner in Winchester? It is safeguarding the gospel that Jesus came from God, because if this is so, something completely new, unique, and with far-reaching consequences has entered their world, our world, your world, my world, making for new preaching, preaching which has a bearing on the lives of all men everywhere—the insurance agent, the nurse, the fitter, the old-age pensioner, and everyone else everywhere and for all time. This good news is what the phrase 'born of the Virgin Mary' safeguards. It says Christ was essentially *different from us*, and yet he became like one of us in order to rescue us from a meaninglessness in life in which it is possible, perhaps even probable, that we shall become lost. For this is our experience, that meaninglessness quickly takes over like the jungle in monsoon lands, when suffering, fear, pain and loneliness break into our routines. But God in Christ has come 'for us men and for our salvation' (as the Creed says), and the phrase 'born of the Virgin Mary' safeguards the essential point that it was God who came, and who still comes in his Spirit, and not merely another man, however remarkable.

Must we still go over the old ground that the Virgin Birth is mentioned in only two of the four gospels and that Paul makes no explicit reference to it, so that a case could be made out for asserting that it formed no part of the original gospel? Perhaps not, but let us not be too sure that Paul was unaware of it, nor too sure that the fourth gospel does not imply it in verse 13 of chapter 1, for the description of the children of God reads, 'not born of any human stock, or by the fleshly desire of a human father, but the offspring of God himself.

9

So the Word became flesh.' Notice the word 'so'. How fitting that this should constitute the text for this sermon. At the end of the first century when this gospel was written, the most 'spiritual' of all the gospels, it was felt that the Virgin birth of Jesus safeguarded the Saviour, pointing to what theologians call his pre-existence as the verse which follows shows. Let us therefore lift up our hearts—God has come to save us.

3 WHAT ACCEPTANCE DOES

Luke 1.27 (NEB) *'The girl's name was Mary'*

We do not know what she looked like. No one knows what she looked like. Not that thousands upon thousands of representations have not been made of her. Indeed, who in all the world among women has been portrayed on canvas by the world's top-most artists and in stone by the world's top-most sculptors, more than Mary, mother of Jesus?—but we don't really know what she looked like.

1 *Intelligence*

But she must have been intelligent. It is difficult to see how she could have spoken out the words of the *Magnificat:*

'My soul doth magnify the Lord: and my spirit hath rejoiced in God my Saviour'

unless she were very intelligent. The structure of the poem is almost perfect and has stood the test of time. Maybe the words have been put into her mouth by St Luke, but whichever way you look at it, Mary has been presented to us as a woman of rare intelligence coupled with poetic sympathy.

And she taught Jesus. In the one-roomed house where they lived in Nazareth, Mary would sit on the floor teaching her small boy. There was no furniture beyond perhaps a wooden coffer where the few treasures were kept, and one treasure would be parts of the Hebrew scripture. You learn from your pupils even if they are under five, indeed, the way to learn is to teach. Think of the questions Jesus must have asked his mother! We may guess that Mary was a very intelligent young woman, and intelligence can be read in the eyes. This much we know then of what she looked like.

2 *Pain*

Was her skin always smooth, her forehead unlined and no crow's feet at the corner of her eyes? It is unlikely. Very soon it was easy to discern pain in Mary's eyes, accepted pain, which is different from resisted pain. It gives genuine character to the face. A general complaint about the faces of those who enter for the 'Miss World' competition is that they are too like painted dolls, devoid of character. One of the faces that has arrested many is that of Edith Cavell, the woman whom the Germans shot during the first world war helping British soldiers escape from Belgium.

It wasn't easy being the mother of Jesus. When a genius gets born into a family the tormenting question for the mother is what will become of him. And at the very outset when Jesus was only a few weeks old, Simeon, with the discernment of long years of experience said, 'This child is destined to be a sign which men reject, and you too will be pierced to the heart.' Not the kind of remark you will easily make to a young mother! But so it turned out. Mother and son loved each other, but there grew to be a generation gap, an intelligence gap and a vocation gap. And in the end Mary saw her son nailed to a cross like some low-born gaol-bird who had fallen foul of the law. She was no mother if she didn't wonder how much better things might have turned out had Jesus taken her advice, if maybe he had stayed a carpenter, stayed in Nazareth, and never got mixed up with top people away from their humble home. All that you would see in Mary's eyes.

Women can have dead eyes, but it is unlikely that Mary's eyes were dead, even after the crucifixion. (I can recall a woman whose only son had had a fatal accident at about the age of fifteen, after which she 'died' although she lived for another forty years. You could read it in her eyes.)

3 *Acceptance*

Women can have bitter, resentful, rebellious eyes. You can observe this in some of the young who take to demonstrations. This is what their hatred (perhaps justifiable hatred) of what they see around them, has done to them. Mary saw terrible things done even to her son, but her eyes were not those of a rebellious woman.

Fortunately we are not left solely to surmise. We read in St Luke's gospel that when this young girl whose name was Mary had it brought home to her that she was to be the mother of the Christ child, aware of the cost to herself in pain for all her association with him, she said, 'Be it done according to thy word.' That is to say, she quietly accepted, she accepted in trust.

Mary's face, we may be certain, and Mary's eyes bore the beauty which shines through pain accepted as somehow in the providence of God. This makes a strong face and a sympathetic face, the kind you can't help noticing.

'In the sixth month the angel Gabriel was sent from God to a town in Galilee called Nazareth, with a message for a girl betrothed to a man named Joseph, a descendant of David; the girl's name was Mary.'

This is a poetic way of describing what is almost indescribable. Let Mary stand squarely before us as a woman above all others. If we Protestants are afraid of Mariolatry—and let us face it, Mary was human and not a goddess to be worshipped—if we are afraid of Mariolatry, let us not be slow in giving this woman all that is due and more.

Mary bore Jesus. Jesus had this woman for his mother. Did they look alike? Could you tell they were mother and son? Did they speak alike? Did they think alike? Did they feel alike? What did Mary give Jesus? What did Jesus receive from Mary?

These are searching questions and many more are locked in the mystery of the Incarnation. But for all that we shall never know the answers; Mary remains to this day as very beautiful with all the depth of meaning that word can carry; because she accepted trustingly what came to her in life, painful though it was.

So the girl whose name was Mary sets up for all time the pattern of the proper reaction to life capable of bearing the name Christian. It is to change what ought to be changed and can be changed, and *to accept what cannot be changed*, as somehow in the providence of God. This is the way of peace in life, of strength of character and ultimately perhaps of beauty too, even for men—we might say, especially for men who are so prone to rebellion. We all need to learn the principle of acceptance.

4 *Application*

What have we to accept? Older people have to accept that they have grown older. This is not easy. The least of the difficulties is a stiffening of the joints, making impossible what used to be a delight. And there is failing sight and a declining fund of energy.

Those in middle life have to accept that on them must fall the burden of carrying responsibility; and women may find themselves having to be a wife to a man, a mother to her children, and a daughter to her ageing parents. This calls for intense watchfulness.

Younger people will have to come to the point of accepting that life will not go all their own way, and that ideals receive rough handling in a competitive world.

But none of us—old, middle-aged, young—must abandon the struggle. We must not reckon that nothing can be or ought to be changed. To refuse to change is to die prematurely. All the same we must learn the principle of acceptance. Some things cannot be changed. This is not resigning oneself to Fate. Fate is an impersonal and non-caring force. Acceptance involves believing that we are in the hands of a God who cares so much that Jesus called him Father and lived by this belief. So did his mother whose name was Mary. She said, 'Be it unto me according to thy word' (to quote the old words). There is no more Christian attitude to life possible, and in practice it turns out to be exceedingly constructive.

4 THE LOST AND FOUND CHRIST

Luke 2.48 (NEB) '*My son, why have you treated us like this?*'

1 *The family confrontation*

Here is a small family of three, father, mother, teenage (or almost teenage) son. The occasion is one of those awkward, even painful, family confrontations when the son has acted independently to the intense displeasure of the parents. So they reprimand him and he answers back leaving them more confused than ever. Truth to tell, they have been confused for months by their son. They thought they knew him through and through—especially the mother. Had she not given him birth? Had she not nursed him and ministered to his every need? Had he not told her everything? But latterly he had been sitting at meals like a stranger. What was the boy thinking? What alien ideas were stirring inside him of which they were in total ignorance? Where did he take himself on those un-explained absences from home? Suddenly the truth dawned on this father and mother—they were losing their son!

This is not a description of a family in Kensington, Kings Lynn or Kettering, though it could be. It is about the Holy Family (as it is called), Joseph, Mary and the boy Jesus. The awkward family confrontation took place in some corner of the Temple at Jerusalem where presumably no one could overhear the sharp words (or were they sad words?) Mary addressed to him, 'My son, why have you treated us like this?'

And his answer back did not help—'Did you not know that I was bound to be in my Father's house?'

All this happened when Jesus stayed behind at the Festival in Jerusalem to hear the debates in the Temple Courts, fascinated. His parents and the large company of pilgrims up for the Festival had left for the long trek home; and not for three days did they discover that he was not among them. Then the anxious journey back to the city looking everywhere. At last they found him, and the awkward family confrontation ensued and the sharp (or sad) words of Mary, 'My son, why have you treated us like this?'

We shall be making a great mistake if we treat this story as wholly unique. Something like this has to happen to every teenage son and to every teenage daughter, and to all fathers and mothers with families growing up. And not only to parents and children but to every one of us. We all have to go through the process of *losing that we may find.* Every person who comes to maturity has to learn what it is to be a good loser. This is what this scripture says.

2 *Three areas of losing and finding*

First, all parents have to lose their sons and their daughters; and all sons and daughters have to lose their parents—*for a while.* There has to be a break from both sides.

During the last twenty-five years the break from the side of the teenagers has been sharp, largely for economic reasons. Having more money in their pockets, they could actually flaunt their independence, which they did largely by wearing outré clothing and deriding the Establishment. It was, it is, immature. Not that their assertion of independence was wrong. The break must be, for unless the young are lost for a while, they will never find themselves. And unless parents are prepared to lose their children, they will not find in years to come sons and daughters who care for them. And the same applies to husband and wife. When a man marries, when a woman marries, a proportion of their freedom is lost. They cannot each act with the same independence as formerly. But a man finds in marriage, a woman finds in marriage, what could not be found without it. There is loss, but there is gain. There is actually gain through loss. The gain is the deepening and broadening of experience with, be it noted, growth in individuality which means unlikeness to each other.

And for all of us, whether young people, old people, married or single, we must all face the fact of losing in life. Losing things is hard. Losing health and strength is worse. Losing those we love is perhaps the hardest of all. But life is so built that sooner or later we all have to lose. Sometimes the occasion is our own fault. At other times it happens apparently by chance or because we are bound into a network of mortality and a network where other people's wrongs and misfortunes affect us. But the Christian gospel announces a gain to be derived from the loss. Not automatically because the truth is not that what happens to us is of lasting—if you like—eternal, significance, but how we face what happens to us. That opportunity you lost! That friend you lost! That standard, that style of life we all have lost as this century has progressed, and there is more to come. There is always a gain to be derived from the loss, *on one condition*, that we accept it without resentment. There is much talk these days about the necessity for all punishment to be remedial, but punishment is never remedial unless it is accepted in the mind without resentment. Always, always, it is the way we face our losses that conditions whether or not there are gains. But there could be gains. Not in the same category, of course, nor on the same level, but in a different category and on a higher level. And it may be that we cannot rise to any height of *spiritual* stature unless we have first suffered losses.

3 *The supreme losing and finding*

We return to the story of Jesus lost for three days in the Temple, and his mother's reproof of his action. 'My son, why have you treated us like this?' There came a time when he was lost for three days again, and everyone thought it must be final. It was the death of Jesus by crucifixion. And Mary cried out again, 'My son, why have you treated us like this?' Why did you not remain in the family circle? Why did you not stay a carpenter in Nazareth like your father? Why did you have to go off on that preaching tour of yours? You saw what happened to John the Baptist when he acted likewise. Why did you challenge the Establishment of your day?—'My son, why have you treated us like this?'

And the Cross stands for ever as the answer to Mary's question, and to your question and to my question, 'Whoever seeks to save his life'—whether by refusing a calling, or by compromise or by downright denial—'Whoever seeks to *preserve* his life will lose it; and whoever loses it will save it, and live.' This is what Jesus said, (Luke 17.33). And Christ's losing of his life was not for the saving of his own soul, but for the saving of yours and mine. He was lost on Good Friday so that he might be found on Easter morning, three days later risen from the grave. This is the good news of Jesus Christ. This is the gospel for us, so that our right action can surely only be to identify with him, for with him no one can possibly be lost for ever.

5 THE NARROW GATE

Matthew 7.13, 14 (NEB) *'Enter by the narrow gate. The gate is wide that leads to perdition, there is plenty of room on the road, and many go that way; but the gate that leads to life is small and the road is narrow, and those who find it are few'*

In Kensington Gardens there is a path as broad as a highway connecting Kensington Road with Bayswater Road and running past Kensington Palace and the statue of Queen Victoria carved by Princess Louise. It is called the Broad Walk. Every weekend it is crowded with people strolling in the gardens, especially in the summer. No one would have the slightest difficulty in finding this footway, it is obvious to all. But there are also narrow and winding pathways in the same gardens, the whereabouts of which would take some describing and even more actually finding. But when they are found, there will be very few people using them.

Some such picture as this Jesus must have had in his mind when he spoke of the two roads as set out towards the end of what we call 'the Sermon on the Mount'. A broad road crowded with people and leading to perdition, and a narrow road with only a tiny handful of pedestrians on it leading to life. And to this picture he added two more features, a wide gate at the entrance to the broad road and a small gate at the entrance to the narrow road. With but a little imagination we can see those gates. The first, imposing, gilded and wide open. The second, ordinary, wooden, and the latch in a place awkward to operate.

The trouble, however, is that the more clearly we see these gates and these roads, the more we dislike this picture. What puts us off is the narrow road and the small gate, not to mention the few people who manage to find them and use them. We have a nasty feeling inside us that this represents an ideal of the Christian life as something exceedingly narrow and the people who profess it, censorious and stuffy. Does the Christian way really have to be like this?

1 *A religion of negatives*

What we dislike about this interpretation is that it largely consists of negatives and this strikes us as unhealthy. Far better life as the German proverb puts it—attributed, whether rightly or wrongly to Luther:

'Wer liebt nicht Wein, Weib, Gesang;
Bleibt ein Naar sein Leben lang'

'The man who doesn't love wine, wife and music, remains a fool all his life'

Puritanism at its worst is very foolish. It cramps people, makes them artificial, and produces a sourness of demeanour which spreads not only gloom in the mind, but can lead to malaise in the body. Most serious of all, it presents a travesty of the good purposes of God for his creation who has 'given us all things richly to enjoy'. Moreover, excessive restriction can produce a reaction into licence. If we need evidence, see how English life developed in the reign of Charles II after the repressions of the Cromwellian period. No, we do not like narrow religion, and if this is what Christ was commending, we would rather have none of it.

2 *Imposed goodness*

There is, however, an attitude even less attractive than this. It consists of one narrow group forcing its ideas of good behaviour on to society at large. It has become something of a feature of this decade. We see little of religious Puritanism nowadays, though it does exist, but there has come into being a kind of social puritanism. It is unlikely that Prohibitionism will be attempted again after the failure in the United States of America in the 1920s, but a similar campaign could get under way against smoking. Excessive smoking is no doubt an evil thing, but we have to be careful not to remove something which in moderation may be a pleasure for some. To do so is narrow. Another area of an entirely different kind where negatives can be imposed is in the public attitude to South Africa. Apartheid is the problem here. It is a bad thing. But is one section of the public right to ban playing cricket with South Africa and to contemplate interfering with postal communications with that country in order to bring home to us all what an oppressive government it is that operates this policy? What we have here is a kind of social puritanism, and into its ranks some would wish to place the social 'do-gooders' who have become a feature of our time. But are we quite sure that this does not display a curious kind of narrowness? And narrowness is not attractive.

3 Denial of self

If the narrow road and the small gate are to be interpreted in this kind of negative way, then it is not surprising if many people reject it. But is this what Christ means? Was he really advocating narrowness? No, this is not so. The narrow road with the small gate which few people find and which leads to life is the one where people put self last.

These 'self-last' people, these selfless people, are not narrow. It is those who see everything from the angle of what advantage will come to them in any line of action, who are the ones who squint through a tiny loophole and see very little of the landscape beyond. Selfless people are generous people, generous in their thoughts about others, generous in their judgements, generous in their attitudes. Self-last people are ready to give and not simply to get. They give of themselves, give of their sympathy, and even of their substance. And they are ready to recognise good wherever they see it, even in most unlikely places.

And this is the remarkable discovery—This self-last approach leads to happiness, such happiness as can only be described as *life*. But few people make this discovery. They think getting produces contentment whereas this result derives from giving. The narrow road and the small gate is the one where self is put last, and those few people who use it find life.

There came a day when Jesus said, 'Whoever seeks to save his life will lose it; and whoever loses it will save it, and live' (Luke 17.33) (NEB). So now we know who these are who are crowding the broad path, they are the ones who are seeking to save their lives by putting self first. And we know who they are who are seeking out the small gate and the narrow path, they are the ones who are putting self last. They lose their life, *but they live*. What is more, they are generous, attractive people. Christ calls us to join this very select company.

6 THE NEW PREACHER

Mark 5.20 (RV) '*And he went his way, and began to publish in Decapolis how great things Jesus had done for him*'

In the modern world this man would receive publicity overnight. Press reporters would track him down to ferret out his story. A microphone would be thrust before his face, and every answer he gave to every question taped on the turning wheels inside the little box the operator carried, ready for nationwide broadcasting the same evening. The man might even be lured into a television studio to be exhibited under glaring lights to a vast viewing public glued to their electronic screens in the corner of almost every sitting room in the land.

1 *The cure*

Who was this man, and why the fuss? This man had been the terror of a neighbourhood. He had been a dangerous maniac, dwelling among the tombs of a grim cemetery on the eastern side of the lake of Galilee, looked upon as heathen territory. No one dared risk passage through that graveyard. Local authorities had attempted crude remedies to tame him, which did not include psychological treatment, but strong chains to keep him in check; but his strength was greater than the strong chains; he broke them, and rampaged the more in consequence of this attempted enforcement of captivity. He would not be bound. He could not be bound. The man was a monster, a bogey man, a threat, we may guess, which stupid parents employed to terrorize recalcitrant children. There were people who had actually seen him, his long, matted hair, half hiding his staring, ferocious eyes; and his whole body filthy and bloody with the gashes he had made upon himself with sharp cutting stones and every now and again roaring out in cries of pain and terror at the internal visions of his own tormented mind.

But Jesus cured him. Not with some weird incantation, but with a word. This was always his way of working, swift, decisive and complete. True, there was a short struggle, for here among the tombs life was encountering death, living death, light was encountering darkness, devilish darkness, the work of God was doing battle with the work of Satan. The demoniac knew this. He knew he had met his Master. He acknowledged it. He attempted to escape impending defeat. But it all happened in a moment. What exactly happened it is hard to tell. Legends built up around the event, especially as at that very time a whole herd of pigs panicked, hurling themselves over the cliff into the sea, to the utter dismay of their owners. But the maniac was a maniac no more. When the locals met him they met a man 'clothed and in his right mind'. There was nothing to say. There sat the man. No-one had seen him sitting before, at least, not sitting still like that. But wasn't there anything to say? There was. The locals came and begged Jesus to leave their country. They did not wish for spiritual power of these dimensions. Better the maniac than this. Religion can be too 'pricey'. And Jesus left the country exhibiting his divinity in doing so, for God does not force his presence on anyone, and his judgements are a ratification of the judgements we pass upon ourselves. If we wish to be Godforsaken we shall be. This is the terror of our freedom and of God's gift of freedom to us.

2 The rejection

Go back for a moment from the cured man to the uncured man; from the freed man, freed from his devils, to the possessed man; from the man sitting clothed and close to Christ, to the wild man, raving among the monuments. Is it possible to be further away from Christ than to be 'possessed'? Yet there are people today, there always have been people, who long for nothing so much as to be 'shot of Christianity and all its works'. Of the inhabitants of Gerasa, east of Galilee, we read in this gospel narrative that 'they began to beseech him to depart from their borders'. They wanted a land evacuated of Christ. These men have their counterpart in the modern world. But does distance from Christ secure liberty? Does a land scoured of religion march forth into the uplands of light? Here we see what happens the further man backs away from Christ. We see what the Germans call an *Unmensch*—a non-man—for what rampaged among the tombs was scarcely recognisable as *homo sapiens*. Taking the road away from Christ is to take the road which ultimately leads to inhumanity. We have seen it happen in Europe in the twentieth century. When a country becomes evacuated of Christ, terror, violence and bestiality clamber quickly over the fences of civilisation. And men open their mouths inquiring—what can have taken place? The answer is simple. Christ has gone because we have asked him so to do.

3 The preacher

But what of the cured demoniac? He became a preacher! Pity we have not more preachers who are cured demoniacs! They might be more convincing in the pulpit! They might testify with more fervour to the gospel they profess to believe having experienced its liberating power in their own persons.

It is true this man was a reluctant preacher. Before he became a preacher he thought up a good life for himself. He would go around with Jesus and watch with open eyes his miraculous ministry. He might even be 'Exhibit A' himself to what Christ could do. This would puff his ego. Such is not unknown in the history of evangelism, or preaching, for that matter. But Jesus refused. The cured man was told to go to his house, (had he really a house?) and tell his friends 'how great things the Lord had done for him.' Home and friends are not the easiest of places to testify. But if we are not prepared to testify to our experience there we had better not testify anywhere else. Even the Apostles after Easter and Pentecost had to start preaching in Jerusalem. Jerusalem is not an easy place to preach Christ, nor was Gerasa, especially as the inhabitants wanted to be 'shot of Christ and all his works'. But this man obeyed. Gerasa was not evacuated of Christ after all. This man combed that hair of his, cleaned up his lacerated body, bought some decent clothes and went trudging through all the Ten Towns (Decapolis), proclaiming the good news of what Christ can do if only we will let him. So he represented the Christ. This is what a preacher should do. It is the heart of preaching.

The Greek word translated 'publish' in our text is normally translated 'preach'. It is a technical word. Perhaps the people in the Ten Towns came to understand this; after all, they spoke Greek there. Any way we ought to understand it, especially if we are preachers in any kind of way. Preaching is publishing the good news of what Christ has done for us.

7 LORD OF THE SEA

John 6.19 (NEB) '*They saw Jesus walking on the sea*'

This is sufficient to cause twentieth-century men to toss aside the New Testament in disgust. 'They saw Jesus walking on the sea.' Not simply standing on it, nor gliding above it like some human hovercraft, but lifting up one foot on the water and putting it down again. This strains our credulity, if it is not also an insult to our rationality. What are we to make of it? Or in more general terms, what are we to do with the miraculous element in gospel stories?

1 *Miracles in general*

We could of course pursue an argument as follows. Miracles do not happen now. We do not see men walking on the sea. Therefore miracles did not take place as described in the New Testament. Therefore the New Testament is unreliable.

Suppose, however, we pursue a different argument. Suppose we recognise that miracles do in fact take place today even if we label them 'faith healings'; they even occur for the non-religious. Therefore the existence of miracles in the gospel stories is credible. Therefore the New Testament is not unreliable.

But we need to be careful. Jesus' miracles do not prove that he was divine, because in the Bible itself miracles are recorded as having been performed by the *opponents* of God's servants. Furthermore, Jesus was a reluctant miracle-worker. There is no trace of Jesus even thinking, let alone boasting, 'I will walk on the sea in order to convince people that I am divine.' Such a notion is grotesque. And Paul disparages miracles altogether, declaring that Christian preaching is in complete contrast to the signs (miracles) Jews seek after and the wisdom Greeks pursue. Instead Paul said, 'We preach Christ crucified'.

So let a positive but open attitude be adopted to the miracles of Jesus. We shall not try to excise them from the gospels. It would be like attempting to keep an umbrella without tolerating the frame. Neither shall we affirm that they did not take place, nor imagine that we are able to explain how the miracles happened, because they would then cease to be miracles. What we shall assert is that the miracles of Jesus illustrate some aspect of what the risen Christ can be to us now. This in fact is how they are set out in the fourth gospel where they are actually called 'signs', signs, that is, of what the real presence of God in our midst *does*.

We must elaborate this point. Miracles are not instances of God breaking into the cause and effect system which we have to rely on in life. After all, where should we be in the engineering world if we were not quite certain that the law of gravitation would always work? No, miracles are disclosures of God's activity within the system of God's created order. God is at work in the miracle of the unfolding rose in the rose garden in June as well as in the migration of birds in the spring and autumn. Looked at this way, the old categories of natural and supernatural are less valuable than the idea of another dimension of being, operating *within* the natural order. So miracles draw back the curtain of sense-perception to show us what the

New Testament calls 'the kingdom of God' in our midst. It was no small part of Jesus' ministry to reveal this new power among us.

2 One particular miracle

And now we turn to the miracle itself of Jesus walking on the sea. The fourth gospel for all its stress on miracles as signs is insistent on describing the historical context of this one. Jesus was under pressure to become a political leader in Galilee but escaped the clutches of the crowd by withdrawing up the hill slopes, and dismissing the twelve disciples in a boat across the lake. It was a time of enormous tension, one lone man resisting the will of a crowd. Then darkness fell, the wind arose, a storm broke, putting the boat with its twelve occupants in dire jeopardy. Then out on the lake, walking on the water, came Jesus.

And now we must enter the mind of these twelve men of Jewish blood despairing of their situation. The Jews hated the sea. They saw it as the dark, irrational, unfathomable abode of all that was evil in the world. The sea was man's treacherous enemy. What then these twelve terrified men saw was Jesus walking confidently *on the sea*. It seems that his intention was to pass them by, to bring about for them a kind of theophany. This is made the more clear by the significant words he shouted to them across the water, seeking to quell their horror at what they were seeing. 'It is I;' (*Ego eimi*—Greek), 'do not be afraid.' 'It is I' refers to the divine presence, and pointing out in these frightening circumstances that 'the Lord sitteth above the water-flood: and the Lord remaineth a King for ever' (Psalm 29.9 BCP), or in the words of Psalm 95.5, 'The sea is his and he made it.' Nothing could be a more striking testimony to the sovereignty of God over all that terrifies than Jesus thus *walking on the sea*.

3 The miracle as a parable

So the miracle becomes a parable. As an historical event, it must evoke a kind of reverent agnosticism. We do not know how it took place. We certainly cannot explain it, but as a parable it has something very needful to say to us. It tells us that there is no situation, however forbidding, however inimical to our peace and safety that Christ is unable to master. The risen Christ does not sink under the troubles of men. It is true, he did once sink. He sank on purpose. He sank for our sake, but he rose again triumphant. This is our Lord. This is the One we worship. This is the One in whom we trust.

Here is a man facing the prospect of redundancy in his employment. This is his 'storm on the lake'. This is where the wind howls and threatens his boat containing his means of livelihood. Is it to be wondered if he cries out in protest? Fear is part of the cause. Fear of the future.

Here is a woman living alone. What happens if she falls ill? What happens if she runs only a slight temperature and cannot get to the shops? There are neighbours, of course. But suppose she contracts a serious illness? Who will take her to the hospital? And what is more problematical, help her over the dragging period of convalescence? There are social workers of course. But these uncertainties are the rough winds she fears, capable of overturning the skimpy craft in which she sails across the waters of life.

And not only are the less well-off liable to storms which threaten their survival, but the affluent as well. Money does not buy off sorrow, domestic tragedy and heartbreak. These waves can wash into anyone's life, undermining what appears to be foundations built to last. But when these personal foundations crack, the superstructure in the business and social world is threatened.

Fortunate in these conditions, and those like them, is the man or woman who can see the Christ coming towards them *walking on the sea*. And not only appearing thus as master of situations, but calling, 'It is I; do not be afraid.'

Does this sound too simple and pretty for a sophisticated society to swallow? But the sophistication of the modern is only a veneer. Underneath are the basic worries about security

27

and significance that have dogged men and women since the world began. The truth is either we trust or we drown. And in the last resort the question is—whom do we trust? ourselves? our luck? money? the Welfare State? The preaching of the New Testament is that our only final security is in God. And what this miracle story shows is that God is not absent from our storm-tossed world but actually in it, *walking on the sea*, the terrifying sea, and calling to us, 'It is I; do not be afraid.'

St Matthew's gospel has an addition to this story. It tells of Peter, confident till he attempted himself to walk on the sea. But 'seeing the strength of the gale he was seized with fear; and beginning to sink, he cried, "Save me, Lord" ' (14.30).

This addition could be our autobiography. At one moment we are confident of our powers, the next moment we are overwhelmed with the terrors that surround us. This is our trouble, we are betwixt and between people, betwixt proud self-sufficiency (apparently motivated by faith, but not really so) and craven fear. We need to grasp the rescuing hand of Christ which means in practice, 'staying our minds on him'.

So this miracle is a disclosure point of the real presence of God in our midst in history with whom we could ride out the stories of our lives and thereby experience the miracle ourselves of Christ *walking on the sea*.

8 A THEOLOGICAL DISPUTE

John 9.19 (NEB) '*Do you say that he was born blind?*'

Here is a man being examined almost as if he were an exhibit in a museum. Was it the miserable wretch whom everyone knew begging for alms of the passers-by? Or was it some-one else very like him? The answer would appear to be obvious, but so unlike is a seeing man to a non-seeing man that to decide is not easy. A man with eyesight looks different, that is to say, not only do his eyes look different, but his whole person. For one thing, he walks differently. And not only this but his clothes are worn differently, and he asks different questions, so that even his voice is different. It really is quite astonishing the differences the restoration of sight brings to a blind man.

So there was a dispute over this man. Had he been born blind or not? And if he had, how did he come to recover his sight? But of course he was not an exhibit in a museum. He could be asked. And his parents could be asked. 'Is this man your son? Do you say that he was born blind? How is it that he can see now?' And they replied, 'We know that he is our son, and that he was born blind. But how it is that he can now see, or who opened his eyes, we do not know. Ask him; he is of age; he will speak for himself.'

1 *The fundamental question*

This miracle story in St John chapter 9 describes the healing of a blind man by Christ at some length. Indeed, in a book of twenty-one chapters, one entire chapter is devoted to this one case. We do well, therefore, to inquire the reason. A blind man begging by the wayside is unlikely to be an influential person, not even when his eyesight has been restored. But the author of this gospel did not record this, or any other healing story, merely for the sake of the miracle, but that it might point to fundamental questions about the man altogether, in other words to act as a pointer or a sign.

What questions then does the chapter raise? Primarily, a probing, hurting question—Are we all born blind? Are we able to 'see' God? Are we able to be aware of the healing power available in the world for every man by the light of nature? Or do we need to have our eyes opened? But who can open this sort of blind eyes? Has Christ the power? Can he do so by the use of material means? Can matter become the medium of restoring spiritual faculties? Is the structured Church an instrument for the recovery of this kind of sight and this kind of blindness?

2 The dispute

These are hard questions and these are disputed questions. So the whole of chapter 9 in John's gospel is cast in the form of a dispute. First the disciples inquired when they observed Jesus with his attention drawn to a blind beggar (probably with a label attached to his person and a beggar's bowl beside him, 'Born blind—earn merit by me'), 'Who sinned, this man or his parents? Why was he born blind?' We can scarcely wait to hear the answer to the question why about suffering, ready perhaps, to speculate about the doctrine of Karma, the transmigration of souls, and much else. But Jesus did not, on this occasion, theologise, he turned at once to practical healing. Making use of a popular, if ineffective, remedy, he spat on the ground, made a paste of the spittle, spread it on the man's eyes, and ordered him to go and wash in the pool of Siloam. The blind man obeyed, and came away from the pool seeing.

At once the dispute flared up. The cured man looked so different that his identity was held in question. Was this the same man or not? And how were his eyes opened? And who performed the cure? There were hard facts to which these questions could be directed. But behind them were debatable questions and debatable answers. Ought this man's sight to be cured at a time in flat contravention of ecclesiastical regulations?

3 The dispute deepens

So the dispute deepened. The cured man for his part was contented to remain agnostic about these religious arguments. He could see, that was sufficient. But questions of this kind do not readily go away. This man believed in Christ's treatment of him sufficiently to be cured, but he was contented to be agnostic about the whereabouts of his healer, and even his identity. So can faith coexist with agnosticism?

The dispute continued, not least because the Pharisees in their rôle as ecclesiastical authorities turned the theological question into one concerning ecclesiastical regulations. This man had been healed on the Sabbath Day! So another question raises its head. Is this typical of the ecclesiastical mind? Does it tend to hide primary questions behind secondary ones?

And then we observe the progressive leaps of faith which this man proceeded to take, even over the barriers of his own agnosticism. Jesus he identified first as 'a man' (v 11), then as 'a prophet' (v 17), then as 'a man from God' (v 33). And in his progress he gained sufficient confidence to question even his ecclesiastical superiors, not without a note of truculence, repeating what sounds like formularies from a catechism learnt in childhood (v 31).

But the dispute does not die down in the chapter, because this kind of dispute never dies down, certainly not when we consider how Jesus built his Church on those who, on his account, were excommunicated from the synagogue. The Jews expelled this truculent half-believer, whereupon Christ found him (v 35), and in being found, the man became not only a full believer, but a worshipper. ' "Lord, I believe", he said, and bowed before him.'

Finally, the curtain comes down on the dispute with the crushing retort of Jesus to the Pharisees' last question (which we also ask). 'Do you mean that we are blind?' and he replied— or at least he replied in words to this effect—'To see what is primary and yet to hide it under what is secondary as more convenient, is damnable. Better a measure of agnosticism with honesty (the blind man), than knowledge with duplicity (the Pharisees).'

The curtain has indeed come down as far as chapter 9 of the fourth gospel is concerned, but the dispute still continues in front of the curtain.

4 *The dispute continues*

Are we all born blind? Are we able to grasp eternal life by the light of nature? Do we need a revelation from God himself before we can even begin to understand him, let alone exercise our faith in him? Is Christ really necessary? Do we need the sacramental body and blood? There are those who are ready to shout negatives. There are the scientific humanists. Man has eyes more than adequate to see his way to a better society without revelation. So the dispute continues, and like the blind man in the story in John chapter 9, we have to make up our minds which side to support.

But when we have come down firmly in believing that man needs a revelation from God himself, which is the answer the Christian must give, we shall still have to inquire if it does not pertain to our mortality that our sight is *always defective*. 'Now we see only puzzling reflections in a mirror', so Paul in 1 Corinthians 13.12, but this will not always be so—one day, 'we shall see face to face . . . knowledge now is partial; then it will be whole.'

We attribute this to our mortality, may it not also be due to the inherent defect in our nature called 'original sin'? which is one doctrine capable of empirical proof. Nevertheless, the message of chapter 9 stands firm—Christ is the restorer of sight to the blind. It is a process which begins in this life and continues beyond the frontier we call death, What a prospect, therefore opens up before us. There will come a day when we shall be able to see with unclouded eyes. Hallelujah!

9 GOD'S PRODIGALITY

'*A sower went out to sow his seed . . .*
some seed fell along the footpath . . .
some . . . on rock . . .
some . . . among thistles . . .
and some of the seed fell into good soil!'

(from Luke 8.5-8 NEB)

At any rate some seed fell into good soil! That is a comfort because the method of sowing employed was chancy, clumsy and wasteful. A man with a basket of seed in one hand and his other employed to scatter it indiscriminately in handfuls! If then this parable of the sower which Jesus told is about preaching, it is eloquent about its wastefulness as a means for informing the lives of men and women with the word of God. Corroboration of this adverse judgement on preaching would not be difficult to unearth in the mid-twentieth century. And Hogarth's paintings of congregations yawning, dozing, snoring or ogling the girls while the preacher droned away in the pulpit, turning the hour glass, do not encourage us to think that preaching was all that more successful in the eighteenth century. But are we right in laying bare this pessimistic view of preaching as the thrust of Jesus' parable? Could it not be maintained that what is being set out here is the optimistic estimate that whatever hindrances the preaching of the word encounters, footpath, rocks or thistles, it will reach a rewarding conclusion in a rich harvest? After all the context in which this parable occurs in Luke's gospel highlights the successful preaching tour on which Jesus was engaged. Crowds flocked to hear him in village after village, town after town.

1 *The wastefulness of preaching*

Yes, but the assessment of the value of preaching must be made, not on whether or not people hear the word of God, but on how they receive it. Some receive it as a pathway receives it. That is to say, they scarcely receive it at all. It merely lies on the surface of their lives. Not that pathways are wicked inventions. Pathways take you to places. They guide you over rough ground. Consult any gardening manual and it will convey the information that in laying out a new garden, the first necessity is to lay down the pathways and they should not be less than two feet wide. So society needs members with minds of their own, people who have hacked out a pathway through life's rough places, and which have got them somewhere. Need we trouble to inquire what happens to the scattered words of a preacher when they fall on the ears of this type of hearer!

Others receive the words of the preacher as stony soil

receives it or thin soil over a rock substratum. It takes root but not deeply. All the same, rock or stone is useful material. With it cathedrals have been built, bridges, monuments, indeed, all manner of structures that require dignity and strength. And even if the rock is strewn over the surface of the land in broken pieces, it serves for making dry walls. We ought therefore not to write off the solid characters upon whom the words of the preacher makes no lasting impression. It is the method that is faulty.

And then the thistle bed at the edge of the field. The very existence of the thistles shows that growth is possible there. Never rule out weed covered land as useless. But merely to toss seed on this ground is hopeless *as a method*. First the ground must be cleared.

So the cry goes up, not least from some clergy, 'In the name of common sense, please cut out the preaching. It is a chancy, clumsy, wasteful method!' Forty years of preaching, wrote Cardinal Manning, after a tremendous ministry as Archbishop of Westminster, is like forty years of beating the air. And perhaps those commentators are right who see in the interpretations of Jesus' parable of the sower as given in the gospel not the words of Jesus himself, but the disappointing experience of preaching by the early Church, as a method of bringing home the word of God to people's hearts.

2 *God's prodigality*

But wait a minute. Are we not rubbing out preaching too hastily? Is not its very chanciness all of a piece with how God works in the world? Look at the operations of the Creator in the natural order. Are they parsimonious? Are they with nice calculations? Are they undertaken with a finicky concern about wastefulness? Is there not a prodigality which astonishes us? Millions of sperms produced to make one life. Seeds formed on plants in profusion of which only the tiniest proportion is carried by the winds or birds to propagate, often in the most unlikely places. Is there not a liberality in God which astonishes us? He makes 'his sun rise on good and bad alike, and sends rain on the honest and dishonest'. May not the preacher then, tossing his words almost recklessly, be in alignment with God's normal method of working?

Or think again how the Word of God was made incarnate in history. Was it displayed in a glass case—housed in some sacred shrine protected by ecclesiastical admission tickets, so that only the genuinely interested should be granted the privilege of his acquaintance? Was it not on the contrary, seen by dirty eyes, if not handled by dirty hands belonging to 'all sorts and conditions of men'? And at the last, when the Incarnate Word was accomplishing his most personal work, most sacred work, yes, most cosmic work, was it not placarded like a hoarding flanking a motorway, a kind of theatron or spectacle as St Paul wrote, of whom only the tiniest proportion could have had the vaguest notion what it meant? The crucifixion of Jesus, the divine instrument for human redemption, was played out close to a pathway, set up on a piece of rocky ground so bare as to remind of a man's shaved skull, so waste as to yield only thistles for its crop, there it was that the incarnate word of God was tossed with apparent abandon as to whether or not any seed would fall into good ground. Which surprisingly enough, some did. One of the terrorists, suffering capital punishment beside Jesus, received the Word with satisfaction, and maybe also the captain in charge of the execution squad, a most unlikely convert.

There are clergy who have accomplished long ministries in which preaching has played an effort and time-consuming part. They could tot up 4,000 sermons preached. Think of it! At the end of the day will they wring their hands and cry, 'To what purpose is this waste?' This labour might have been spent more profitably in social services to the underprivileged, echoing you will note, the statement of Judas. But who knows what results have been achieved? Who knows where the word of God has become rooted and productive as a direct result of one of those sermons, heard, maybe, by unpromising ears. Fortunately, we do know of some results, less impressive no doubt, than the case of D. L. Moody, whose Sunday School teacher threw in her hand because she assessed as worthless her ministrations with that urchin in her class; and less impressive than the words of the faltering lay preacher in Colchester whose miserable congregation that morning happened by chance to contain C. H. Spurgeon. Yet many a common run of clergyman knows of lives remade, wounds healed, even sacred ministries undertaken because of some words scattered in preaching, without the knowledge exactly of where they would fall, and how they would be received.

3 *Preparatio evangelica*

Preaching then is not to be excised from the Christian ministry. On the other hand, it must not be allowed to function as an isolated ministry. The professional preacher has no place in Christian service properly understood. Preaching is a part, but only a part of the pastoral office. Need the question be asked, what success would attend the labours of any farmer if he only concentrated on sowing his seed? Attention needs to be given to the soil. In a way this is laborious, unexciting work. In the garden it may well mean double digging, and in the fields turning out in all weathers with the plough, the harrow and the roller. Expense, too, will be incurred for composts, fertilizers and drainage. All of which being interpreted means that the Christian minister cannot neglect the indisputable fact that it is the good soil that produces the harvest. It is there that the seed germinates. So the environment in which men and women grow up is important. Adequate food supplies, housing, education, in short the social services are not outside the province of preaching the gospel. *Preparatio evangelica* they may be, but they are no less necessary for being so.

'And some seed fell into good soil.' After our preparations, our *preparatio evangelica*, we shall reckon we know where exactly that good soil is and we shall plant our seeds just there. But sometimes God has the last laugh and the best growth takes place in the patches of ground we wrote off as hopeless.

We had better be prepared. God has a way of cutting our boasted expertise down to size. Wisdom counsels that whatever else we undertake we go on scattering the seed.

10 THE LIGHT OF LIFE

John 1.4 (AV) *'In him was life; and the life was the light of men'*

Imagine for a moment a club-room. It could be in St James's, London, an officer's mess at some army barracks, or even a saloon bar in a country town. The members sit around for the most part talking, but there is no animation, no excitement and very little expectancy—until all of a sudden the door bursts open, and there strides in a man with an arresting personality. His zest for living and his strength of character mark him out from the general run of men, and not only these obvious qualities, but his buoyant, engaging and at times teasing conversation. When he enters it is as if all the candelabra have suddenly been lit by an invisible hand.

1 *The light of personality*

Was Jesus of Nazareth this kind of personality? Is there not in these words from St John's gospel an indication of some such man as this—'In him was life; and the life was the light of men'? In the Christian Church we are so familiar with the Cross as the distinctive Christian symbol, which, indeed it is, that we have come to think of him as pre-eminently the man of sorrows. But is this a true picture?

In his book *The Door Wherein I Went* Lord Hailsham* has this striking passage:

'As I reflected upon this, I came to the conclusion that the first thing we must learn about him is that we should have been absolutely entranced by his company. Jesus was irresistibly

* (Collins 1975) pp. 55, 56.

attractive as a man. The man whom they crucified was intensely fond of life, and intensely vital and vivacious. He did not wish to die. He was the last person to be associated with suffering. They called him a winebibber. They abused him for the company he kept. What was it, do you suppose, that kept Mary at his feet when Martha was scurrying about getting the dinner? Was it a portentous commentary on Holy Scripture? I feel sure that it was simply that she found his company actually enthralling. When one begins to think of it, can one see anything but fun in calling the two enthusiastic brothers 'Sons of Thunder'? Or impetuous, chivalrous, heroic, but often blundering, Simon, the Rock? Is there no hint of humour in the foolish virgins, or the unjust steward, or the camel who finds it impossible to get through the eye of a needle, or the comparison of the speck of dust and the great beam in the eye, or the picture of wicked old Tiberius getting back the penny with his ugly old face on it, or the mustard plant likened to a tree, or the Trade Unionists who complain at the end of the day that someone else has got by with only an hour's work for the whole day's wage? Once one reflects about this, the picture of Jesus suddenly comes to life. The tragedy of the Cross was not that they crucified a melancholy figure, full of moral precepts, ascetic and gloomy. He was not John the Baptist, and the Baptist acknowledged this. What they crucified was a young man, vital, full of life and the joy of it, the Lord of life itself, and even more the Lord of laughter, someone so utterly attractive that people followed him for the sheer fun of it, someone much more like the picture of Dionysius in a Greek mosaic than the agonized and broken figure in a medieval cathedral, or the Christos Pantokrator of an orthodox monastery. The man of sorrows acquainted with grief was in himself and before his passion utterly and divinely joyous. The twentieth century needs to recapture the vision of this glorious and happy man whose mere presence filled his companions with delight. No pale Galilean he, but a veritable Pied Piper of Hamelin who would have the children laughing all round him and squealing with pleasure and joy as he picked them up.'

Or think of Jesus' style of talking. Don Cupitt in a Radio talk published in 'The Listener'* said,

'He uses irony, humour and stories to awaken perception. He ridicules our painfully literalistic understanding of God by directing us to think of God in ways he, and we, know are absurd. In one story, he tells us to think of God as a lazy judge who cannot be bothered. We have got to keep nagging at him. Elsewhere though, he says just the opposite: don't keep nagging in prayer. The parables solemnly assure us that bad men are good and good men are bad. One story tells us to admire a spend-thrift, another a swindler, and another one an outcast. The method of Jesus' teaching is to evoke a sense of God by the use of irony and paradox. His method is not literal or dogmatic, but always oblique. He uses the same stratagems against himself: "Why do you call me good?" "Who made me a judge over you?" He calls himself a servant, not a Lord, the very least in the Kingdom of Heaven. Jesus' message was indirect and ironical, in a way that makes the standard Christian doctrine of him as a straight incarnation of God seem very flatfooted. It eliminates his subtlety.'

2 *The inner light*

Of course we cannot stop here. The text, 'In him was life; and the life was the light of men', has far more depth in it than an indication that Jesus of Nazareth was a captivating personality but it is a place to begin. We do not, most of us, indeed cannot, start with the philosophical or even the theological. We must make contact at the human level, and this is what the enflesh-ment of God makes possible. Creative life and the experience of light—and their interdependence—are not, for the most part, mediated to us by means of abstract ideas, but by a man who talks and laughs and intrigues all the time he is at it, till we find ourselves inquiring what is this life and light, only to learn that it is what God is, and not only what God is, but that by which everything else is—the eternal Word, the Logos.

* London, 15 July 1976.

This depth of meaning the New English Bible conveys when it translates the Greek as 'all that came to be was alive with his life, and that life was the light of men'. So Christian eyes are carried out and away to a grand principle of interpretation far beyond pedestrian forms of religion. Every man, not simply the Christian man, every man has within him the light of life—Jew, Greek, Mohammedan, Hindu, Humanist, Agnostic and Atheist—every man exists because the Logos exists, the Eternal Word as it were, 'lights him up'.

In the Leicester Evening Mail of 19 May 1944 there appeared this story. Two stretcher bearers, Private Elwood and Bugler Hunt, were returning to their lines on the Arakan front with a casualty when they heard a rustling in the bushes and the click of a rifle-bolt. Out into their path stepped a six-foot Japanese with a rifle at the ready. He looked at the two men and the third man they carried on the stretcher, and then without a word or gesture dropped the muzzle of his rifle and stepped back into the jungle.

Was he a Christian? It is possible. More likely it was a case of a non-religious Japanese living up to the light which lightens every man who comes into the world. We know what mercy and truth are and that they should be practised.

Se we recognise two lights in the world which are really the same light but seen in two places, the inner light possessed by every man and the outer light incarnated in Jesus Christ.

3 The Light of Christ

In the fourth gospel, the same gospel from which our text is taken, we have this sentence, 'Once again Jesus addressed the people "I am the light of the world. No follower of mine shall wander in the dark; he shall have the light of life." ' If it is difficult to conceive of anyone announcing, 'I am the light of the world', especially anyone who like Jesus was bent on living as a servant among his fellows, and said so, then refuge may be taken in what most New Testament scholars assert, namely, that the fourth gospel is a reflection on the significance of Jesus to those who believe in him. *Christians have found Christ* to be the light of the world because in actual fact (however humbly he lived out his life on earth) that is what he really was and is, the light of the world.

But what does this mean, Christ is the light of the world? Does it mean that the whole world was totally dark before his coming? No. Does it mean that no light shines at all in civilisation and religions other than Christian? I think not. Does it mean that Christ brought in a completely new scheme of morality and that we do not know what moral values are apart from him? No. What Christ provides is light upon what we already half know and half attempt and half long to carry out. What Christ's coming does is to turn up the lights in the half-lit rooms in which we already move, giving us power to achieve what is otherwise impossible.

Let me illustrate. Here is a young married couple with two children. By no stretch of the imagination could they be described as affluent, but they were happy, gloriously happy in their unpretentious home. And then the war of 1939 broke out and the husband was called up. For some time the separation was bearable because he was based in Scotland and there were fairly frequent leaves. Suddenly on the other side of the world the Japanese bombed Pearl Harbour. Thereafter the young couple's life changed for the worse. The husband was posted to the Far East. Weeks dragged on, then months, no news came. At last the dreaded message 'Posted missing'. The wife struggled on. There was nothing else to do but struggle on. A home had to be maintained for the children and it had to be a happy home for their sakes. So after a fashion she lived, perhaps existed would be too strong a substitute for 'lived', but there was no mistaking the fact that she had lost the light of her life. And then one day, one astonishing, stupefying, miraculous day, there stood her husband in the room with her, only weeks after she had received a notification from the War Office that he had been taken prisoner and was now released. Is there any necessity to describe the transformation that took place in that woman's life? Cannot we all guess? But do not miss the point. She still had to peel the potatoes for dinner. She still had to struggle to clothe the children in their most expensive years. There were problems about modern living to which she could find no answers. But she could accomplish all now because the light of her life was with her.

So it is with the coming of Christ into our world. No quick answers, no simple answers, perhaps no answers at all are given to the economic, social and political problems we face today, but in the light of the sacrificial life of Christ we are given a new perspective which alters everything. People are seen differently, money is seen differently, race is seen differently, failure is seen differently, yes and even death as well. So the drag departs, the depression and the utter disillusionment. 'In him was life, and the life was the light of men.'

4 Reflected light

We are supposed to be lights in the world. Jesus said to his disciples in his sermon on the mount (as we call it): 'You are the light of the world.' Is this possible? Is it presumptuous? Not if we understand the light we provide as reflected light, light reflected from living with Christ. But we must let it shine. It is utterly wrong for Christians to spread gloom in their dealings with people. And this means the home as well as the club, the pub or the office. When a Christian enters every place should be at least one degree brighter, Why? Because reflected light has entered, light from the life of Christ who is the light of men.

11 CHRIST'S STRANGE STRATEGY

Matthew 10.16 (NEB) 'Look, I send you out like sheep among wolves; be wary as serpents, innocent as doves'

There exists, and always has existed, what must surely be described as an inferior method of Bible study. This consists of employing the Bible as a kind of puzzle. The student tots up the number of times fish are mentioned, or reptiles, or precious stones, indeed, whatever happens to take his fancy. Here then is a verse replete with treasure for this style of investigation. Four members of the animal kingdom are listed in one sentence, 'Look, I send you out like sheep among wolves; be wary as serpents, innocent as doves'—sheep, wolves, serpents, doves. What a collection! What a menagerie!

And this colourful assembly stands in. St Matthew's gospel as Jesus' way of describing the nature of his commission to his twelve apostles. Moreover, since those twelve apostles represent the Church of Christ for all time, this colourful message is applicable to all whom Christ sends forth to fill out the mission to mankind which he initiated. This means bishops, priests and deacons, ministers and missionaries of every kind, and not only they, but all baptised Christians who have confirmed in their own personal commitment the faith which the Church confesses, that is the Christian minority in every community, including housewives, shop-keepers, professional men, secretaries and school children, every one who accepts the name Christian, 'Look, I send you out like sheep among wolves; be wary as serpents, innocent as doves.'

1 *A strange strategy*

But what an extraordinary strategy! The temptation is to label it ridiculous. 'Look, I send you out like sheep among wolves.' Do not miss the strength of the wording. '*I* send you out.' *Ego apostello* is the Greek original with the emphasis on the 'I'. Let there be no misunderstanding. This is Christ's intention for his servants. Sheep among wolves. 'Poor sheep' we complain, 'What a hope!' Need we show surprise if some opt for this strategy *in reverse*, 'Look, I send you out as wolves among sheep.' Some Churchmen have in fact so acted, and if some of our minds rush off to the Renaissance Popes, can we be blamed! But no, Christians are to step out from Christ's presence into the world as sheep among wolves.

2 The wolves

The wolves exist. They prowl around among our industrial workers, intelligentsia and 'submerged tenth'. Their aim is subversive. They seek to tear society apart. They plot and plan to overturn the structure of the community as we know it. One of their tools is 'sexual liberation', so called. If the family pattern which forms the basic unit of the community can be broken up, a disintegrated society will not be long in following. So sexual intercourse outside marriage is popularized and pornography assessed as therapeutic. Two consequences follow. Revolt against traditionally accepted morality leading to revolt against all forms of authority, not least the law and the police. And secondly, a permissiveness in sexual standards encouraging a laxity about all standards together with a loss of discipline. The wolves operate a cunning subterfuge and they work over the whole field of public life concentrating on education and everything which conditions public opinion. They are organised. They are clever. They are ruthless. They are bent on devouring all that has been influenced by Christian values. This is the tough world in which the Church lives today. Do not underrate the opposition. Jesus never fell into this trap.

3 The need for attack

The temptation of course on the part of all of us who own the name of Christian is to retreat or opt out. Or if this is unthinkable, then to huddle together in some form of ecclesiastical ghetto, to hide behind church walls, Church tradition and Church language. And the result is a siege mentality and a fortress mentality, forgetting, if we ever knew, that the only safe form of defence is to attack. This is what the early Church did. It out-thought the hostile pagan world of its day. So ought the Church to be doing now, striving to out-think the pseudo-intellectualism which opposes its gospel, taking care lest activism become a substitute for thought. It requires engagement with the world, not retreat from the world. 'Look', said

Jesus to the twelve, 'I send you out' (*apostello*). 'I send you away from the flock into the world.'

4 *Life style*

What is to be the life-style of Christians when they are engaged on their mission? Two instructions are provided.

First, they are to be 'wary as serpents'. The Authorized Version reads 'wise as serpents' and this translation of *phronimos* is not wrong. We need wise men, learned men, scholarly men, and men full of experience related to their scholarly learning. Christian leaders neglect their books at their peril and at their followers' peril. The reference, however, is not first of all to book learning, but to watchfulness, and it applies to all Christians, not only to leaders. There is a need for alertness and a readiness for quick reaction.

Think of a snake. Some of us may never have seen a snake. This would not be true of the Apostles. A snake lies basking in the sun, perhaps on a rock, apparently asleep or even dead. But touch it and its fangs will be in you in a flash, almost before you are aware of it, or if it is a small snake, it will have disappeared before you can turn round. Christ's representatives are to" be conscious that they operate in a dangerous world. They must not be lulled into a false security. There is hidden danger abroad. There are traps for Christians, dangerous mantraps. Know about them! Watch out for them! Use your intelligence! Do not get caught!

Secondly, 'innocent as doves'. The Authorized Version has 'harmless' instead of 'innocent'. Perhaps 'straightforward' is a possible translation. Doves are unlikely to be labelled as innocent by the gardener who has seen what they can do in a row of greenstuff in a vegetable plot. But doves do not attack anybody. They do not harm other living creatures. And with their pearl grey plumage they are beautiful to behold. It is no wonder they are a symbol for goodness, and in the Bible the symbol for the Holy Spirit of God. In the prologue of St Mark's gospel we read that the Holy Spirit descended on Jesus 'like a dove'. All of which surely cries aloud this message of scripture that we, Christ's followers, Christ's servants, Christ's men and women, are to be conspicuous for our goodness, which does not mean being simpletons, naïve or lacking in expertise. Against such an interpretation the foregoing attached phrase is a safeguard—'wary as serpents'. We might have conjectured that since crafty rapacious wolves prowl about our world, force and craftiness ought to be the life-style of our calling—but no! The only effectiveness we operate in the long run as Christ's representatives is Christlikeness or *goodness*.

There came a day as recorded in the book of the Acts of the Apostles, when the same twelve men whom Jesus commissioned stood in the prisoner's dock at Jerusalem, charged with preaching in his name. But no charge could be preferred against them. Therefore, embarrassing as it was, their captors could do nothing but release them. Why? Because they were powerful, dangerous or clever? None of these things, but because it was plain for all to see that they intended nothing for the people among whom they worked, but what was good and wholesome.

> Sheep among wolves,
> wary as serpents,
> innocent as doves.

Application

Gifts, skill and standing we may as Christians possess, and they are not to be despised, yet what will finally count is none of these assets, but our goodness. Yet it is not really our goodness, but a reflected goodness, Christ's goodness reflected in us, reflected in us so long as we keep in his company, even as the twelve apostles were called in the first place in order that 'they might be with him'. (Mark 3.14 AV and RV) We shall go out into the world as

> sheep among wolves,
> wary as serpents,
> innocent as doves,

but we should not fail to return to Christ again and again lest in due time we have no light to reflect in an overcast world. Out from Christ. Back to Christ. This is the strategy, *his* strategy for *his* Church. We shall do well to observe it.

12 THE CLOTHES OF JESUS

Ought a sermon be preached about clothes? The reaction to this question might be that clothes are a trifling matter unworthy of the serious consideration of a Christian preacher. But do not clothes concern people? Do not food *and clothing* represent the fundamental necessities of human life? We cannot exist without food. We cannot exist without clothes. And clothes form a large part of women's world, with the result that fortunes are made in the realm of fashion. Dior and Hartnell are names with which to conjure.

Clothes are an indication of personality. There is a firm of tailors which displays the advertisement, 'clothes make the man'. If this is true, so is the reverse, 'the man makes the clothes'. As for men so for women. Some people can wear almost anything and appear striking. Others can put on the identical garments and be scarcely noticed.

How did Jesus wear his clothes? Maybe we have given little thought to Jesus' clothes. But they are mentioned at least five times in the gospels. At the outset we are told that he was 'wrapped in swaddling clothes and laid in a manger'; and at the end that he was wrapped in linen clothes and laid in the tomb. At birth and at death clothes are insignificant because we do not choose them or really wear them. But when we are in the full flush of adulthood they assume importance. It is worth noting, therefore, that we are not left in complete ignorance about clothes at this time of Jesus' life. There are three references. There was the woman with the haemorrhage who crept up behind him in the crowd in order to touch his clothes. There was the occasion in the courtroom the night before his crucifixion when the soldiers stripped him of his clothes and arrayed him in comic garments. And there was the moment when the executioners at his cross cast lots for his clothes what each should take.

This last reference may serve as a starting point to consider what were the clothes Jesus wore. Since there were four soldiers in charge of the crucifixion and the clothes of the victim were by tradition the perks of executioners, they had a problem. Like most other men, Jesus wore five pieces of clothing. One garment apiece then, but what about the fifth? Tear into four parts? But it looked too good to tear. So they tossed for it. Thus one soldier went home with Jesus' undergarment, a seamless long coat worn next to the skin, perhaps woven by his mother. Did he show it off to his wife or his girl-friend? It is impossible not to wonder what became of it.

But what were these five pieces of clothing? First there was the 'chiton' already mentioned. Then there was the girdle tied tight around the waist so that the chiton billowed out above it providing a kind of commodious pocket in which food was placed, or in the case of shepherds, lambs carried 'in the bosom'. Attached to the girdle was a purse and a pen and ink for a scribe, and a dagger in the case of the desperadoes. Over this alb-like garment a cloak (himation), was worn out of doors. This was the third article of clothing. The fourth was the headdress, consisting of a close-fitting felt or cotton cap (rarely removed), and a piece of white or coloured cotton, perhaps a yard square, folded to make a triangular piece and laid on the head with the apex backward, the whole kept in place with a rope-like circle of camel's hair. Fifthly, there were the sandals.

1 *His own clothes*

Consider now the three significant occasions on which the clothes of Jesus are mentioned. First, the occasion when a woman suffering from a twelve-year haemorrhage edged her way through the crowd breaking the law every moment by the contact she made as she jostled her way, but bent on one aim—to touch Jesus' clothes. We leave aside considerations as to the proportions of faith and superstition in her attitude, and consider those clothes that she touched. Were they simply clothes? Was that 'himation' on which her fingers rested merely a few square yards of brown material? No, they were *Jesus'* clothes. They were the clothes of the Saviour, the clothes, as it happened, of *her* Saviour, for she was healed when she touched them.

There is a true story of an American preacher whose influence on the lives of people was widespread, deep and lasting. This man possessed a hide-out bungalow away from the city where he worked, in which he and his wife relaxed as opportunity afforded, and found physical and spiritual refreshment. Often they had to rush back into the city because of the urgency of some pastoral call, leaving the bungalow just as they were living in it. There came a day when it happened as often before, but this time the tragedy was that he met with a fatal accident, leaving his wife heartbroken. But she had, one day, to steel herself and return to the bungalow where they had been so happy, in order to arrange for its sale. What, however, overcame her completely was the sight in the bedroom of her husband's slippers just as he had kicked them off. So it was an article of clothing that conveyed most poignantly the reality of the person.

Clothes are an indication of personality but by reason of their association with the wearer they can be more, they can be conveyors of the resources of personality. That is to say, clothes are not only signs of what a person is, they can be effective signs making a presence felt in absence. Every bereaved husband or wife knows that the hardest task after a death is to dispose of the clothes.

Can we use this incident to understand a little more of what sacraments are, especially the sacrament of the Body and Blood of Christ? The material elements are the effective signs of Christ's presence. They are the means by which we make contact with him, and the means by which he 'comes over' to us. Sacraments are much more than the clothes of Jesus Christ, but they are like his clothes. He has chosen them and

49

made them his, and by them we recognise with whom we have to deal.

'If I may but touch his clothes I shall be healed', said the woman with the haemorrhage. What risk there was of magic, what risk of superstition, what risk of sheer irrational sentiment. All this is true of the sacraments, but power flowed through the woman's touch of even his outer garment, the 'himation', because it was *his himation*.

2 *Comic clothes*

Consider next the flogging of Jesus in the yard at the back of Pilate's judgement hall on Good Friday morning. The soldiers were not satisfied with raining blows on the prisoner's back. They wanted fun from the occasion. And so they stripped him of his clothes, his himation, his chiton, his girdle, his head-dress, his sandals—everything. Jailors learned before this Good Friday and since, that one way to break down a prisoner's resistance is to reduce him to the indignity of nakedness. The Nazis did this, and Communists likewise. But these soldiers went further. They redressed Jesus in comic clothes to make him appear a ridiculous king. Then they mocked what they saw.

There is a deep truth here. These men did not mock the real Christ. They mocked instead the caricature they had devised. They put clothes on him that did not belong to him. Perhaps this is done to Christ more frequently than we think. Maybe it is often done unwittingly. It could be that the Church has done this time and time again throughout her history, perhaps is doing it today—misrepresenting Christ to the world by word, by attitudes and by ecclesiastical structure. And men mock. But they are not mocking the real Christ but a mis-representation of him. And some misrepresent Christ *in order* to mock him, and all for which he stands. This is worse.

Whatever the reasons, what we see here is the ridiculed Christ. We see Christ as a comic king, Christ as a figure of fun, without his proper clothes. So Christ takes his stand alongside all the outsiders of this world, the mis-shapen and clumsy, whose highest level of attainment can only be that of a circus clown, wretched at heart, people for whom there is no fun because people only laugh *at* them, people who are the butt of everyman's comic approach.

But note this, before Jesus was led out to be crucified, they redressed him in his proper clothes. So people recognised the Jesus they knew on the way to his cross. Clothes, and the way we wear them are an index of identity.

3 *Stripped of his clothes*

And now the third reference to Jesus' clothes, how they were stripped off by the soldiers. What we are not told is that some one else must have gone about wearing Jesus' sandals, and someone else his cloak, and someone else his tunic, and someone else his headdress, and someone else his girdle. We do not hear of any miracles wrought by those articles of clothing. There is no magic of this kind in the gospels. When the woman who touched Jesus' clothes received healing, it was because hers was the touch of faith. Without the faith neither clothes nor sacraments bring healing to those who make contact with them.

So Christ's clothes were lost. How priceless today would be even one of those sandals or part of the rope of camel's hair that kept his headdress on—but there is nothing, nothing for money to purchase, nothing for superstition to handle. Christ left only one remembrance and this was a symbolic action. 'Do this in remembrance of me.' And he took bread and poured out wine. So today these sacraments are the effective, material signs of his healing presence. They are the only clothes (so to speak) that remain. How wise then, how salutory, that we should treasure them. This is what counts, and it is here that Christ shows the way.

Mark 11.12-14 (NEB) *'On the following day, after they had left Bethany, he (Jesus) felt hungry, and, noticing in the distance a fig-tree in leaf, he went to see if he could find anything on it. But when he came there he found nothing but leaves; for it was not the season for figs. He said to the tree, "May no one ever again eat fruit from you!" And his disciples were listening'*

1 Spiritual hunger

Here is a story. It is only a story but it is not without a basis in fact. It concerns a young couple whose only child died soon after he was twelve months old, and it was not possible for the wife to have another. They really were heart broken. Lacking any kind of religious faith as a sustaining power, purposelessness and meaninglessness gradually overtook them. After a time their marriage grew shaky till finally in desperation they visited a Marriage Guidance Counsellor. She was a wise woman whom they met, and she recommended that they seek out a personal faith for themselves, and to do so by joining a Church. By this time they were hungry, spiritually hungry. They did not resent the advice given, on the contrary, they set about attending their local church. It boasted a reasonably large congregation, the ceremonial was impeccable, the music almost of a professional standard. But although they gave it a fair trial, no warmth of fellowship ever touched them, nor did any word from God to people who knew they had lost their way ever reach them. So they left off church-going. Had they known their New Testaments, which of course they did not, they would have recognised themselves in the story of Jesus being hungry and making for the fig-tree in leaf, hoping to find something, but when he came to it he found nothing but leaves.

It is not easy to conceive of Jesus as physically hungry, dependent on the chance prospect of finding sustenance on a way-side fig-tree, so sheltered (we must suppose) and so forward on account of an unusual spring, that it was prematurely in leaf and might therefore be bearing premature figs as well. And if this physical hunger is difficult to conceive, how much more difficult to think of him as hungry for spiritual sustenance in the Temple worship of his day and finding it offered nothing but outward ceremonial, legalism and party strife.

2 *A difficult story*

But did it happen? Did Jesus curse a barren fig tree? There are those who cannot surmount the apparent problem involved in this incident (if it actually took place), in order to begin to appreciate the parabolic teaching which it presents. What harm had the fig-tree done that it should be cursed and condemned to death? And was it not unreasonable to expect figs on a tree when the season for figs had not yet arrived? And what are we to think of a religious teacher so frustrated by what he finds that he breaks out into a curse! And that of a tree! So this scripture presents itself as a stumbling block to some who would like to believe, and as a stick to beat the Church for others who have no desire to believe.

What answer can be given to these questions? Perhaps the ruthless one that the incident being out of character did not take place. But can we arbitrarily presume to judge scripture in this fashion? Perhaps the tempting answer, because it neatly side-steps the problem, is to assert that here we have an acted parable. Jesus was performing a symbolic act as a prophet completely in character with some of the Old Testament prophets, notably Isaiah walking naked and barefoot (20.2-5), Jeremiah burying his girdle (13.1-7), and Ezekiel cutting off his beard and dividing it into three parts (5.1-4). But then this Markan scripture distinctly says that Jesus approached the fig-tree in leaf *because he was hungry*. Nevertheless there are no incomparable difficulties in accepting the narrative as it stands. And that one tree should be caused to wither away 'from the roots up' (v 21) is no more detrimental to a belief in the divine ordering of nature than that millions of elms in Southern England should be allowed to perish from Dutch Elm disease. At the same time to accept the incident as historical in no way exhausts its significance. There are lessons to be learnt here.

3 The lessons from the incident

The overriding lesson is one of warning. God looks for results from religion. A cultus is not an end in itself. That this story of the cursing of the barren fig-tree is broken in the middle by the account of the cleansing of the Temple by Jesus, shows up sharply what is the lesson. Christ rejects all religion which has ceased to provide a way of access to the living God. He condemns it. He goes further, he foretells its coming destruction. As in the parable of the barren fig-tree recorded in St Luke chapter 13.6-9 (which may have shaped the recording of this event in St Mark), he asks 'Why should it go on using up the soil?' Make no mistake, however, Jesus did not reject organised religion as such, he rejected organised religion which produced no spiritual results.

What were those results? *First*, prayer. 'My house shall be called a house of prayer for all nations' he insisted. What is prayer? Prayer is opening up the life to another dimension. It exhibits humility. Men and women are not self-sufficient. It contains also an attitude of expectancy. Whoever lifts up his hands does not come away empty-handed. It is true God may not put into them the expected, nor even what is asked, but those who ask do receive, those who seek find, and to those who knock there is an opening of the door. Religious practice should be the place where traffic between God and man, man and God, is conducted, not a place for traffic between men and men with merchandise.

Secondly, there should be faith. When the next morning Jesus and his disciples took the same road as on the previous day, on which the barren fig-tree was cursed, the disciples drew his attention to the way in which it had withered from the roots up, and he replied, 'Have faith in God', and continued, 'If anyone says to this mountain, "Be lifted from your place and hurled into the sea", and has no inward doubts, but believes that what he says is happening, it will be done for him. I tell you, then, whatever you ask for in prayer, believe that you have received it and it will be yours.' For Jesus faith, like prayer, was the means of making contact with God, indeed, faith and prayer, prayer and faith, go hand in hand. What they do is make God's power, God's almighty power, available. We have not begun to understand religion as Jesus understood it unless when we pray we believe we are doing precisely this. Prayer is opening up a situation for God, and when this happens mountains of difficulty no longer constitute irremovable barriers. All this we listen to with patience, half-believing, half-doubting, till Jesus turns on us with a stern warning which shocks us—I tell you this, unless your religion does exhibit faith as one of its chief products, it is a useless encumbrance, fit for destruction.

Thirdly, religion should produce power. This scarcely needs arguing because it is the corollary of prayer and faith when understood as opening up the human situation to the coming of the divine presence. And when this occurs, the kingdom of God is present, and when the kingdom of God is present, things begin to happen. So it was in the ministry of Jesus. The blind were given sight, the lame walked, the deaf heard, and the poor had the gospel preached to them. No doubt we need to be careful how we look for results. We may be looking for the wrong results, the spectacular results, the results that will make us proud of our Church membership, and be disappointed that we do not see them, when all the time God is making seeds grow secretly in most unexpected places.

4 Application

In the year 1556 in the reign of Queen Mary, Cardinal Pole succeeded Thomas Cranmer as Archbishop of Canterbury. He planted some fig trees in the courtyard at Lambeth Palace which are still there, or at least trees derived from the original seedlings. They are vigorous trees producing each year a profusion of rich green foliage. But not only foliage but figs in abundance. Of those trees it cannot be said that they are never 'nothing but leaves'.

But what of the Church of England of which Lambeth Palace, the chief residence of Archbishops of Canterbury, is a symbol? What of our own local parish church? What of the place of worship we attend, be it Anglican or some other denomination? What of our own personal religion? Is it largely a thing of externals? Is it conspicuous for representing a mere conformity to tradition? Does it really make any practical difference to our conduct and attitudes? And has it any effect on our community? What can we *show for our faith*? If nothing at all, Christ has no use for it. He even prophesies that it will wither away. Only the religion which makes it possible for God to work through people has any future, but if it does make this provision it is never outmoded, never irrelevant and never withers away.

14 CHANGING SIDES

John 18.5 (NEB) '*And there stood Judas the traitor with them*'

They could scarcely believe their eyes. Through the trees of the garden a sizeable posse of soldiers was advancing. There was no mistaking their identity or their mission, they came with lanterns, torches and weapons. They were out to take Jesus by force if necessary; perhaps his followers into the bargain, if the opportunity arose. For some moments they stood there lined up awaiting orders. Then it was that the horror of the situation clarified epitomised in one short, sharp sentence in the fourth gospel. 'And there stood Judas the traitor with them.'

Do not miss the point that throughout the ministry of Jesus all who encountered him were constantly being urged to take sides. The gospel of the kingdom which he proclaimed did not look for men and women to halt between two opinions, but to choose whom they would serve, which meant *either* taking sides with Jesus and the disciples who gathered round him *or* taking sides with the Scribes, Pharisees, Sadducees and Herodians who stood over against him. Judas was among those who gathered round Jesus, so close in fact that he stayed in that company almost until the last hour, even partaking of the Last Supper; but now suddenly there he was on the *opposite* side, standing in with the soldiers, come to arrest Jesus, obviously leading them. The disciples could scarcely believe their eyes, but 'there stood Judas the traitor *with them*'.

1 *The Divisive Christ*

Sooner or later all of us must come to recognise how Jesus is a divisive person. He spoke about this himself (Matthew 10.35 AV) 'I am come to set a man at variance against his father, and the daughter against her mother, and the daughter-in-law against her mother-in-law. And a man's foes shall be they of his own household.' This need not surprise us. Weak men and colourless men evoke neither protest nor approval, they are either pushed to the wall or pass unnoticed. Jesus, however, was a strong personality, a colourful man, 'a city set on a hill that could not be hid, a lamp set on a lampstand'. And as if his very existence was not in itself sufficient to polarize people, he went on to make it gritty with the obtrusive question 'What is your opinion about the Messiah? Whose son is he?' All this divisiveness the fourth gospel summarised as follows, 'Here lies the test: the light has come into the world, but men preferred darkness to light because their deeds were evil.' (3.19) (NEB)

Since the first world war in Britain there has come about a sharper distinction of what a Christian is than existed in the Victorian and Edwardian eras when church-going was fashionable. In those times to refuse to make this confession would have been counted eccentric, even preposterous, if it did not indicate Jewish blood or some 'heathen' religion. The whole country was Christian. The majority of the people was baptised. But today a member of the House of Lords, someone on the team of the popular BBC programme called 'Any Questions' or a journalist writing in the most reputable section of the press, will be counted a brave man if he makes the declaration, 'I happen to be a Christian.' So society is divided in the twentieth century, divided by Christ. Some are on his side, some stand over against him, and a crowd hovers in between, halting between two opinions, displaying in consequence the inevitable impotence which hesitancy engenders.

There are those of course who attempt to side-step the embarrassment of taking sides. They affirm that religion is a private affair which indeed it is, but it must be a strangely ineffective affair if it can have no public consequences. And some are loud in their assertions that a man does not need to attach himself to a church in order to be a Christian, which again is indeed possible, but not with great hope of maintaining his identity as such. The blunt fact is that Christ called men and women to stand in with the group that acknowledged him as 'Master', and if necessary, to be counted, and the call still operates today.

2 The identity of the traitor

Who then is Judas? Judas is the man who changes sides. 'And there stood Judas the traitor with them.' Judas is the man who has lived as a recognised member of the Christian Church, a hearer of Christ, a doer for Christ, and one who has partaken of the Holy Communion. Judas is not an outsider. He is an insider. Bishop Richards in a fascinating exposition of St Mark's Gospel called 'Jesus—Son of God and Son of Man' has suggested that if, as is possible, Judas was the only Judaean among the twelve apostles, he knew his way around Jerusalem, and so it was he who was entrusted with the task of arranging for the ass to be available for Jesus' triumphal ride into Jerusalem on Palm Sunday; he it was who made the advance preparations for the Last Supper to be held in an upper room with which he was acquainted. Certainly he was no rustic ignorant of how to approach the high priest in person, or too conscious of social inferiority to undertake diplomatic overtures. Clearly he who was seen leading the posse of soldiers to the garden of Gethsemane was no man without 'savoir faire' in the capital city itself. Judas was someone to be reckoned with, who had openly joined the embryonic Church of Christ and been recognised as a trusted member.

But now the horrible truth stares the remaining eleven disciples in the face as the soldiers with lanterns, torches and weapons burst into the garden and draw up under the trees— 'there stood Judas the traitor with them.' One of their number has changed sides.

What made him do this? Was it money? The priests to whom Judas sold Jesus knew better. Thirty pieces of silver was a laughable price for one whom they would have been ready to half empty their coffers to be rid of conveniently. Was it jealousy? Peter, the man from the fish-wharf in Capernaum, given the primacy in the apostolic band over this intelligent, personable man from the south? This is too simple an explanation. Was it that Judas could suffer the passive rôle Jesus had apparently chosen for himself no longer? Jesus, he saw, had in him what it takes to be the leader of a nation; the nation urgently needed a leader at this time, indeed camouflaged in hiding places throughout Judaea and Galilee were desperate men with forbidden arms, waiting for the opportunity to arise in revolt against the accursed *status quo*. All they wanted was a leader, and Judas saw that Jesus had it in him to be their man. He would himself follow Jesus to the death if need be, if only, yes, if only, Jesus would abandon his ridiculous meekness. And so he tricked the chief priests into letting them think he was betraying his Master; the thirty pieces of silver scarcely interested him, it was a detachment of soldiers he wanted. When Jesus saw these he would rise to assume national leadership and those crowds who lined the route to Jerusalem on Palm Sunday would fall in behind. So Judas attempted to force

Jesus' hand. He reckoned he knew how Messiah should act. Far from a cross being inevitable, a crown was inevitable, if only, yes, if only, Jesus would exert the powers he undoubtedly possessed. But Judas' subtle plan—if this was his plan—miscarried, and when in the garden Judas saw that Jesus *intended* to continue his submissive way and *let himself be taken*, he knew the game was up and hurried off to hang himself.

Judas was no fiend, no devil with forked tail masquerading as a man. Judas possessed such qualities as to cause Jesus to select him from a crowd to be one of his chosen twelve companions. And Judas, for his part, was devoted to Jesus. The kisses in the garden on the night of the betrayal were not wholly false; but from being a follower of Jesus, he had become exasperated with Jesus, and from being exasperated, he came to the point of deciding to correct the meekness he could no longer stomach. Not that he was the only one of the twelve who felt this way. Peter himself made the attempt at Caesarea Philippi and was called 'Satan' to his face by Jesus for his pains. Nor is this the only similarity between Peter and Judas. Peter denied Jesus, and Judas betrayed him. There is not all that much difference between denying and betraying. Judas, however, went to extraordinary lengths to make Jesus go his way, the way of the world, the way of violence, the very course of action Jesus had foresworn in his temptations. So Judas changed sides. Instead of following Jesus as Lord, he tried to lord it over Jesus. Instead of being Jesus' disciple, he attempted to become his master. And as a result when the soldiers filed into the garden of Gethsemane at the very moment when, in an agony of prayer, Jesus was accepting death by crucifixion as the will of God for him—'there stood Judas the traitor with them'.

3 *Manipulating the truth*

The temptation *to manipulate Jesus* is always with us. Sometimes it takes extreme forms as when anti-Semitics, to justify their own views, attempt to prove that Jesus was not of Jewish origin; or when practising homosexuals try to persuade us that

Jesus also was homosexual; or when men wishing to overthrow existing situations by means of violent action, posit Jesus as a political Christ. These are all manipulations of Jesus.

And there are those who try to *manipulate truth* for their own ends, who argue that pornography is beneficial, that work is a four-lettered word, and that law and order is subversive of human happiness. The *Little Red Book* is an example.

And there are those who deliberately set out to manipulate people, to get them where they want them so that they can exploit them, or crush them or ridicule them, or use them as play-things, casting them off when they are finished. Pimps, procurers and the organisers of houses of ill-repute fall into this category, as well as the promoters of sweated labour and all kinds of slave traders since the world began.

Does all this seem a far cry from us. The answer is 'yes', until it dawns on us that we could change sides. We could join the people who assert today that there is no life beyond this life, no standards that are absolute, no power operating in the world beyond that which man wills. We 'insiders' who on no account could be labelled 'bad', but who even partake of the Holy Communion, we could go and stand on the opposite side with those who deny all those things in which we have believed. There is that in Christian faith which is attractive and there is that which offends, and this latter part is pinpointed in the Cross of Calvary. This is the stumbling block. This is what Judas would not accept, and what Peter nearly did not accept. Here then the message. Do not change sides because of what you do not like about the road which Christ took. If you will have him at all you must have him as he is. You must take him as your Master.

15 HUMILIATION

Matthew 16.22 (NEB) 'No, Lord, this shall never happen to you'

It was near Caesarea Philippi, outside Galilean territory, that Jesus began to let his twelve disciples into the secret convictions of his own mind, that he was destined for the gallows. It was shocking news. Shocking, not simply because Jesus was an innocent man, but shocking because (at least in the mind of Peter) he was the Messiah, even more, he was 'Son of the Living God'. But how could God be killed? God who actually *is* life, the fountain of all life. Jesus' sombre intimations did not make sense. How could they? And so 'Peter took him by the arm and began to rebuke him: "Heaven forbid!" he said. "No, Lord, this shall never happen to you." '

So Peter, with the best will in the world, attempted to protect Jesus. We Christians do likewise. We have made the attempt recently. We have heard of a Dane called Thorsen and his intention to produce a film of the supposed sex-life of Jesus, pornographic in style. So we have been up in arms. Petitions registering protest have been drawn up bearing signatures that must have totalled thousands upon thousands. Questions have been asked in Parliament. The Queen herself has made a statement. Yes, we have men risen in a body to protect Jesus from the filth of a sex-ridden decade. 'No, Lord, this shall never happen to you.'

1 What the Incarnation involves

Have we acted wrongly? But how could anyone who bears the name of Christian take no action when people's noblest instincts have been offended by such a film as this? What decent man alive is there who would stand idly by, for example, and hear his mother called a 'whore'? The trouble with our Western world is that it has let reverence disappear, denying that there are some things which are simply 'not done'. One is to besmirch innocence. Another is to destroy irreplaceable works of art. And yet another is to steal away the ideals by which individuals manage the pilgrimage of life. The twentieth century has witnessed too much deliberate irreverence, and now Jesus of Nazareth is being subjected to this same shabby nihilism. No wonder we rush to his defence. 'No, Lord, this shall never happen to you.'

But sometimes in our zeal for what is pure, lovely, and of good report, we act unwisely. There are those now in the present opposition to Thorsen, who, in order to protect Jesus from pornography, assert that he had no sexuality. Centuries ago the early Church Fathers made this claim. They asserted that the human nature which Jesus assumed in his Incarnation was human nature before 'the fall', that is to say, human nature without sex, because sex is an index of fallenness. Fortunately, Gregory of Nazianzus demolished this mistaken theology once and for all, with his pointed phrase, 'That which has not been assumed has not been healed.' After all, if Jesus did not put on our human flesh as we know it, how can he possibly have come to rescue us from the situation we are in? The truth is— Jesus was a male. How else are we to read Luke 2.21, 'Eight days later the time came to circumcise him'? To allegorize here is to become ludicrous. And if we hesitate, let the Epistle to the Hebrews direct our thinking, 'It is not angels, mark you, that he takes to himself, but the sons of Abraham. And therefore he had to be made like these brothers of his *in every way*.' (2.16, 17). To be a man and not an angel is to be a sexual being, and to be a sexual being is to know temptation in this department of life. So the writer of the Epistle to the Hebrews continues, 'For ours is not a high priest unable to sympathize with our weaknesses, but one who, because of his likeness to us, has been tested *every way*, only without sin.' (4.15). We must, therefore, be careful, lest through a mistaken zeal for moralism, we falsify the truth about Jesus as the New Testament presents it, and posit him as some kind of being who *seemed* to be a real man, but who was not. So we fall into the old heresy called

Docetism. This is the wrong way to protect Jesus. 'No, Lord, this shall never happen to you.'

2 Degradation chosen

There came a day, however, when Jesus *was degraded*. That is to say, the thing about which Peter protested so vehemently, taking Jesus by the arm, actually took place. What is more, Jesus took no steps to prevent it happening, which is why he rebuked Peter for the protest he made. Jesus did not intend to be protected from degradation. He purposed to walk into it, believing it to be his Father's will for his life. Of course he shrank from the terrible prospect. He was a man with nerves like the rest of us. We may suppose more sensitive than most of us. No wonder that his praying in the garden of Gethsemane only hours before it took place was a nightmare. Even so, he did not turn back. And when morning came he was exhibited on Pilate's balcony before a gaping crowd as some kind of comic king with that ridiculous crown of thorns on his head, *thoroughly degraded*. This was what *he chose*. And as if this were not enough, Pilate introduced him with the words, 'Behold the man!' And what sniggers, cat-calls and jeering went up from the crowd at that moment, we are left to guess.

Jesus was degraded. Jesus chose to be degraded. He put himself in the company of all those whom their fellow-men and women down the ages have degraded, including those whom pornography degrades today. Because this is what it does. Pornography reduces human beings capable of lofty ideals and heroic actions to the level of creatures with sexual organs and little else—in 'hard porn', not even beauty.

3 Representation and Redemption

There are two points to observe. *First*, Jesus identifies himself with the degraded. He represents the degraded. And curiously enough, the Thorsen film has underlined this precise ministry of Jesus, showing us that whenever any man or woman is degraded, Jesus is degraded in the process, for he represents humanity—he is 'the Man', man as he might be and could be. Pilate spoke more truth than he knew when he said, 'Behold the man!'

And *secondly*, Jesus chose to be degraded, not only to show us that in degrading anybody we are degrading him, but actually to take upon himself man's sin of degrading his fellows, so that he might take it away. This is the mystery of Christ's redemption of mankind.

> 'He was wounded for our transgressions,
> he was bruised for our iniquities:
> the chastisement of our peace was upon him;
> and with his stripes we are healed.'
>
> (Isaiah 53.5 AV)

'No, Lord, this shall never happen to you.' But it did happen. And if we have eyes to see, we must thank God that this was so. While therefore we rightly protest about Thorsen's projected film and seek to prevent its production, let us not be shocked over it more than we are over the fact that Pontius Pilate, Caiaphas, and the Judaean crowds degraded Jesus long ago; and not more shocked than when any man or woman is captured and degraded by our modern pornography for financial gain; rather let us see in Jesus pilloried by the suggested pornographic film how low he stooped to identify with us in order that he might redeem us. And then maybe we shall bring ourselves to the point of not only protesting, but praying for Thorsen as we can be absolutely certain Jesus would have done.

16 OUR LIMITATIONS

Luke 23.26 (NEB) *'As they led him away to execution they seized upon a man called Simon, from Cyrene, on his way in from the country, put the cross on his back, and made him walk behind Jesus carrying it'*

It was not far that Jesus had to carry the cross on which he was to be executed, only a few hundred yards, but it was too far for the strength that remained in his body. He sank down in the roadway under the weight. And no wonder. He had sweated blood the night before, resisting temptation, then the sickening betrayal, then the arrest, followed by the trial dragging on through the hours of darkness, and not long after daybreak, the cruel flogging by brutal soldiers at Pilate's command— no wonder he sank down on the *via dolorosa*. He had reached the limit of his physical resources. If his cross was to be carried at all, someone else would have to do it for him.

1 *Accepting limitation*

But why preach about this? Why make more of it than of some wretched prisoner in some labour camp east of the Urals, falling with frost-bitten feet on the hard road, unable to stagger another yard towards the factory? Why make more of it than of some widow, making her way at first light across London Bridge to clean offices in the City morning after morning till she collapses and finds herself in hospital, nervously and physically exhausted? Why? Because Jesus was the Christ. That is why. And since he collapsed on the job of fulfilling his divine work of redeeming mankind, it is clear that he had no resources to call upon other than those available to us all; he was in the same human category as that prisoner beyond the Urals, or that frail woman crossing and recrossing London Bridge. Jesus had limitations beyond which he could not go.

If then the Christ himself had to come to terms with limitation, is it any great surprise that we are called to do the same? There is a widespread resentment today about any form of personal limitation. There always has been but at a time when human rights have been widely campaigned—and with reason—people tend to resent any form of disability. But limitation is of the very essence of being man and not God. All men have limitations. But the limitations are not evenly distributed. That is the rub.

Here, for instance, is a grown-up version of a thalidomide baby—how will this man cope with life? Here is a woman with an irremovable birth-mark on her face. Here is a boy from a broken home. Here is another born in a family with hereditary mental instability. Here is a girl who simply lacks the academic ability of her sisters—the list of limitations which people suffer could be endless We all have limitations, not so drastic as these, perhaps, and not so obvious, but there are more people who suffer some hidden disability than appears on the surface. Some have innate (as opposed to acquired) homo-sexual inclinations. How do we face our limitations? With resentment? With open rebellion? With insistent demands for public sympathy and special treatment? Of Jesus it is recorded that he carried his own cross without complaint, and when women by the roadside loaded on him their sympathetic grief, he refused it gently but firmly. Jesus did not canvas for sym-pathy. Doubtless this is an elementary lesson to learn from Christ's passage to his cross, but it needs to be learnt. We must accept our personal limitations without resentment and without demanding special treatment if we would follow in the steps of Christ our Lord.

To accomplish this is hard. If we think otherwise we have not known what affliction is, certainly not as Simone Weil plumbs its depths in her book *Waiting on God*, using the word *malheur*, which carries an undertone of inevitability and doom. Probably in our human strength and weakness we cannot adjust to it, but as St Paul reminds us, God's grace is sufficient, and his strength is made perfect in our weakness. In the light of this we can accept limitation.

2 Receiving assistance

There is, however, another lesson to be learnt from this incident. We must be willing to accept assistance when it is offered. Some people find this extremely difficult. They are prepared to give, but they cannot receive. This was not so with Jesus. Moreover, he was willing to receive assistance from a stranger. After all, who was this Simon from Cyrene, coming in from the country on whose back the cross was lifted? Was he a Jew? Was he so little aware of what was going on that day, or so little interested that he was coming *into* Jerusalem, when most people were going *out of* Jerusalem, in order to witness the execution of this man Jesus, whose name was on everyone's lips? Was he a moral man? Was he fundamentally an irreligious man? Apart from the fact that he had two sons, Alexander and Rufus, we know nothing for certain about him; nor, we may suppose, did Jesus. Yet he received the help which came from this anonymous man, no doubt with gratitude, pressganged though he might be into doing what he did.

Being willing to receive is a large part of Christian discipleship; which is why proud men, and rich men, and intellectual men, and women too, (though perhaps with less difficulty at this point), do not easily become Christian disciples. Humility is required, confession of weakness and even repentance. God's salvation is something which in the first place has to be received, it cannot be earned. 'Receive the body of our Lord Jesus Christ which was given for you, and his blood which was shed for you' are the words of the priest in the sacrament of the Holy Communion. There is nothing else possible then but to extend the hand to take. And if we wish instead to earn our salvation we never find it. Christians must be humble enough to be receivers or they will not become Christians nor stay Christians. This too is what the story of Jesus receiving assistance from Simon of Cyrene has to tell us.

3 Sharing Christ's redemption

But in our exposition of this incident so far we have not really penetrated to its subtle significance. Remember Jesus was on his way to accomplish his great work of redeeming mankind; indeed he was already accomplishing it as he was treading that hundred yards or so to the place of execution. We are accustomed to think of him as carrying out this cosmic work alone. He was the faithful remnant of One who, as our representative, offered the sacrifice of perfect obedience to God. All had forsaken him and fled.

Jesus did not, however, accomplish his redeeming work alone. It was shared by Simon of Cyrene. Only to a minimal degree, we may protest, but it was shared. Does this mean then that some of us by our suffering share the load of his suffering that makes for the redemption of mankind? Is this what Paul implied when he said that we make up the sufferings of Christ? Is it possible in the light of this scripture which tells of Simon, helping Christ to redeem mankind by carrying his cross *for him*—we repeat, is it possible to see that the apparent pointlessness of that prisoner stumbling with his frost-bitten feet on the way to the factory may not be pointless after all? And that widow woman's exhaustion brought about by crossing London Bridge to clean offices day after day, may not be entirely purposeless after all? It takes faith, of course, to redeem sufferings such as these, but is not such redemption possible? The real hurt in pain is its apparent senselessness.

Go deeper. This man Simon was pressganged by a tyrannous political power into carrying that cross. Could this by any chance mean that the sufferings of innocent people brought about by the oppressive powers of police states may somehow be contributing to the redemption of the world? This is no argument for doing nothing to help oppressed minorities, nor an argument for tolerating oppressive regimes, but is it a possible light in an otherwise blanket of thick darkness? For the sufferings of men and women since the world began raise a terrible question mark over the rationality of the universe and the almightiness of God.

Let us bring the matter home. That neuritis of yours which will not let you sleep at night. That son of yours who has broken up his marriage. That physical deformity which will not allow you to enter into life as others have entered into life. Each one of these is a limitation. Each one a negative in itself. Could it be made a positive? Could it be offered in faith to Christ as part of his sufferings for the redemption of the world? Could it be your lifting along the *via dolorosa* of life the Cross of Christ which he pre-eminently carries? Simon did it though he was not consulted. Neither have you been consulted. More troubles have fallen upon you. But you could carry them this other way. That is to say, you could, by the grace of God, and then what a transformation of tragedy there would be.

17 NAILED TO THE CROSS

1 Corinthians 1.23 (NEB) '... *but we proclaim Christ—yes, Christ nailed to the cross*'

It is a ghastly subject. The mind recoils instinctively from any man who could bring himself to exhibit so repulsive a scene, even though only in words. A dead man, twisted by torture, every bone protruding from his bruised body, his tongue too swollen for his mouth any longer to contain it. Blood, sweat and excrement exuding a stench offensive to all but the flies which settled in droves. No one who ventured to gape at a crucified man ventured again. This however is what St Paul made the centre of his preaching—'but we proclaim Christ— yes, Christ nailed to the cross.' Perhaps among modern representation none brings home its obscenity more than Frank Roper's Crucifixion in Bronze.

Why did Paul placard this gruesome picture? What made him set a horror in the centre of his preaching? Was he reacting, as some painters reacted in the 1920s and 1930s against anything attractive in the conventional fashion? Or as twentieth-century novelists reversed the happy endings of Victorian romances? Life is an untidy, messy, complicated affair. How could it appear otherwise to a generation that had dragged through the miseries of trench warfare and the holocaust of the Battle of the Somme! But was Paul reacting? Was he not rather pioneering? What religion before or since has depicted God as a pain-drenched figure?

But perhaps we have read the New Testament wrongly. Perhaps we ought not to see 'Christ nailed to the cross' as the central proclamation. Perhaps we ought to look to the Sermon on the Mount, or to the Discourses in the Upper Room or to St Paul's eulogy of love. After all, if we wish to uplift we display uplifting pictures, tell uplifting tales and inspire with uplifting thoughts. Did not Paul himself write, 'Whatsoever things are true, whatsoever things are honest, whatsoever things are just, whatsover things are pure, whatsoever things are lovely, whatsoever things are of good report; if there be any virtue, and if there be any praise, think on these things.' (Philippians 4.8 AV) But the facts are that at least one-third of the total gospel records are devoted to the narratives of the death of Jesus, an affair so disgraceful we might have expected it to be dismissed in two sentences—but it is not. And Paul himself wrote, 'God forbid that I should glory, save in the cross of our Lord Jesus Christ' (Galatians 6.14 AV) and 'I determined to know nothing among you but Jesus Christ and him crucified' (1 Cor 2.2). We cannot, if we study the New Testament, avoid the conclusion that 'Christ nailed to the cross' is the overriding theme of the entire book, whatever we may think about its propriety.

There are some well-meaning, indeed thoughtful Christians who resist this and claim that the *resurrection* of Jesus is the heart of the New Testament proclamation and not 'Christ nailed to the cross'. This is a mistake. Granted that without the resurrection there is no gospel, but Christ did not die in order that he might be raised; rather he was raised in order to set God's seal on the fact that he who died was the Lord. No, the cross was the place where the battle was fought and won, and the resurrection tomb was the place where the spoils of that victory were gathered in. Or to put the matter another way, 'Christ nailed to the cross' is the redeeming event and the resurrection is the interpretation of it. Speak then of Good Friday and Easter as one event if we must, but do not overlook where the centre of gravity lies, it is at Calvary, it is 'Christ nailed to the cross'. And if our old liturgies were at fault in almost omitting the resurrection, our new liturgies are at fault if they have shifted emphasis away from the cross.

2 *What the cross says*

What then does the proclamation of 'Christ nailed to the cross' say? It says Christ became a reject, a reject from society, yes, from religious society, even more from God himself, 'My God, my God, why hast thou forsaken me?' It is not possible to be more of a reject than was Christ, or more of a 'throwaway', or more of an alien. Yet this is what the New Testament proclaims. Let the message be expressed harshly, roughly and crudely, so that its true colours are evident—Christ, the kicked-out man! We repeat, what does this proclamation say?

It says there is no place of rejection in which a man may find himself where Christ has not already been and still in spirit occupies. The extraordinary fact is that men know this when they find themselves trapped in desperate circumstances of a physical kind. Visit some of Europe's medieval prisons and there will be seen scratched on the bare stones representations of the cross of Christ. No doubt some of those same prisoners also cursed God, but at the end of the day when they were utterly alone it was to the battered Christ they opened their appealing hearts. Or turn to a great Muslim mystic and martyr, Al-Hallaj. When his executioners were hacking off his hands and feet, he called for God's mercy on his executioners (can there be any doubt?) with 'Christ nailed to the cross' in the forefront of his mind. This was AD 932. Or come to our own day, to Palestinian refugees and a volume of modern Arabic (that is Muslim) poetry, associating the tragedy of these people with the figure of Jesus crucified. Not that the poet sees in the cross any kind of redemption but rather the shame of victimisation. But this is the point, wherever men are in pain, rejection and tragedy, the One felt to be at hand, despite barriers of race or religion, is 'Christ nailed to the cross'.

So what does the proclamation of 'Christ nailed to the cross' say? It says, there is no place to which a man may come where God with his love is not. It says that to be separated from the love of God is impossible. For a time a man may think he is cast off. Agonising in some physical pain he may imagine that God has abandoned him to the terror of hell, but it is not so. Christ goes to hell with him! Or, sick with himself in that he has sunk to levels of indecency, which most of his life he has abhorred, a man may reject himself, wipe himself off, but Christ does not reject him, he was and is a reject himself! Or a man may come to the point of utter weariness as he sees scheme after scheme for the betterment of society fail, and give up in despair. Christ stood and still stands in the place of heart-breaking failure! We repeat, it is not possible to be separated from Christ—'Who shall separate us', wrote Paul in one of his finest outbursts, 'Who shall separate us from the love of Christ? Shall tribulation, or distress, or persecution, or famine, or nakedness, or peril, or sword? . . . Nay, in all these things we are more than conquerors through him that loved us. For I am persuaded, that neither death, nor life, nor angels, nor principalities, nor powers, nor things present, nor things to come, nor height, nor depth, nor any other creature, shall be able to separate us from the love of God, which is in Christ Jesus our Lord' (Romans 8.35-39 AV). The truth is we cannot be alien to Christ because he himself was and is an alien. So he is with us. That is what 'Christ nailed to the cross' proclaims.

3 The nature of sin

And now we are in a position to weigh the fact of sin. What is sin? Sin is a thing which separates us from God. It may be sodomy. It may be such exploitation of labour that only the word slavery will suffice. But it may equally well be spiritual pride or plain thoughtlessness. But it separates. To say this is sufficient. Therefore it is sin and it alienates, and sinners are those who live in a state of alienation from God.

Alienation, however, from himself is what Christ does not

allow. He became an alien himself not through law-breaking, but through being broken by the law, he let himself be engineered into the seat of the alien. So the separating wall between Christ and the sinner is broken down by him. And this is what the forgiveness of Christ means, allowing nothing to stand between himself and the sinner. Just as if two men in business had clashed seriously because one had stolen business from his partner by an underhand deed. But he owned up to it. And the offended partner spent all night agonising over the hurt he had suffered, but in the morning he went forward with outstretched hand, bruised though he was, and allowed nothing to stand in between their partnership in the days that lay ahead.

This then is what 'Christ nailed to the cross' proclaims. Christ forgiving our sins by breaking down the walls that separate men from God and God from men. 'God is reconciled to us', be reconciled to God. In other words, 'Look, I have not rejected you. Do not reject me.'

4 *The golden cross*

And now the cross with Christ nailed to it begins to look different. It looks different because we begin to see it with different eyes. Barren of meaning it is ghastly. A dead man twisted by torture, every bone protruding from his bruised body. But when we hear the new preaching which goes with it we begin to see the glory. And instead of representing it with dark, gnarled beams of wood, we make it a shining thing of fine wrought gold, studded, maybe, with precious stones. Why? Because that cross is precious, precious to God, precious to man. It promises a final home-coming to every man in whatever far country he finds himself. It proclaims a new ethos to the community, a way of forgiveness, partnership and peace. And it causes to spring up in the beholder a correspond-ing spirit of reconciliation. No wonder 'Christ nailed to the cross' constitutes the new preaching from the New Testament. It is that in response to which there issues what can only be called newness of life.

18 AN ASSESSMENT OF JESUS

Luke 24.19 (NEB) *'A prophet powerful in speech and action before God and the whole people'*

Were they right? Had these two travellers on the road to Emmaus made the correct assessment of Jesus of Nazareth?

1 *A prophet*

First of all, was he a prophet? Did he belong to that unique lineage of men in ancient Israel who proclaimed what God was saying in the face of contemporary decadence, apostasy and rebellion? Did he speak words of judgement as well as words of mercy? Did he employ startling language? Poetic language? Symbolic language? Was the content of his speech radical, provocative and disturbing?

How can we deny these identifications that Jesus was a prophet? Did he not tear away with devastating words and unanswerable logic the religious superficiality which cloaked the hypocrisy of his day? So ruthlessly indeed that those who provoked a dialogue with him broke off the conversation and assembled instead to plot his murder? So it comes as no surprise to hear his cry at the end of his life, 'O Jerusalem, Jerusalem, the city that murders its prophets and stones the messengers sent to her!' And no surprise to hear him continue, 'How often have I longed to gather your children as a hen gathers her brood under her wing, but you would not let me.' So we have it—the word of judgement, but the word also of mercy; the word of condemnation, but the word also of promise. This is true prophetic utterance. The judgements of the prophets were always conditional. If men will turn from their evil deeds and make their way back to God, God will forgive; more than that, he will gather them to himself and care for them, for in his heart he has never ceased to love them. Yes, Jesus was a prophet.

2 Powerful in speech

But these two travellers had more to say than that he was a prophet. They asserted that he was powerful in speech. How is a man powerful in speech or 'mighty in word' as the Authorized Version translates the original? Certainly the reference is not to the volume of his voice. Doubtless Jesus had thought deeply about Isaiah 42.2 (NEB) which tells us that God's servant does not 'call out, or lift his voice high, or make himself heard in the open street'. Jesus was no ranter, rabble-rouser or bawling market-square demagogue. He was gracious in speech (Luke 4.22 NEB) and gentle in manner. But there was no flabbiness about his utterance. What he said was not cluttered up with empty clichés. He did not pad his sentences with verbiage, nor did he chatter, nor labour with an impediment in his tongue. We may guess that he spoke only when he had something to say, and then and at once results followed.

3 Powerful in action

So Jesus was powerful in speech and action. The speech and the action are to be coupled together. Here we have what the Grammarians label a 'hendiadys', that is, one thing described by means of two things. Jesus' speech was part of Jesus' action. He acted by speaking. His speaking effected changes. It was therefore effective speaking and creative speaking, revolutionary speaking. Nothing was ever quite the same after Jesus had spoken. A paralytic was healed, a possessed man exorcised, a tax-gatherer impelled to follow him, and a house of mourning filled with the peace of God. Through Jesus' words there followed the power of God. This was because he lived in the closest union with God. Words are expressions of what we are. They are extensions of our personalities going out to reach other people, and other circumstances. Men and women in touch with the power of God convey the power of God when they speak. Empty people produce empty words, producing results, if any, empty of positive results.

4 A speaker before God

Still we have not quite plumbed the depths of the estimate of these two travellers to Emmaus on the first Easter Day about Jesus of Nazareth. They said he was 'a prophet powerful in speech and action *before God and the whole people*'. Notice the phrase 'before God'. How does one utter effective speech before God? What does the phrase mean? Surely that Jesus' speech never partook of 'playing to the gallery'. To do so is ever the temptation of the gifted speaker. Those who fall into this snare utter words to impress, to inflate their own ego, to hear and bathe in the applause they know they can win, to parade wit, cleverness or learning. This kind of speech can be amusing. It can also be cruel. Jesus could face God with his speech because he was utterly honest with it, whereas liars, flatterers and deceivers cannot, at least they cannot get away with it. Jesus 'set a watch before his lips', he never spoke to the people with his back turned on God.

5 A speaker before the people

Yet he did also speak 'before the whole people.' He came out on the stage of public life. He was not a silent servant of God. He did not assert that his bearing as a man of God would suffice, or that his deeds would suffice, he spoke *before* the whole people. Had he refrained from this what an impoverished ministry his could have been! His words were not only informative, didactic and directive, they were conveyors of the grace of God to heal, restore and forgive. Nor were they restricted to the inner circle of the faithful, the appreciative family of God's people or the *cognoscenti* among them, they were proclaimed where the whole people could see and hear.

Yes, these two travellers on the road to Emmaus had thought out their description of Jesus of Nazareth, they had got it right, or nearly right—'he was a prophet powerful in speech and action before God and the whole people.'

'Nearly right', I said, but they were in ignorance about one utterly decisive fact which made Jesus more than a prophet, more than an effective speaker, more than a public benefactor with words. They did not know that Jesus had to die and that the death was the great part of his ministry, his resurrection included. Yet had they but reflected on one of the greatest of the prophets, if not the greatest, Jeremiah, they would have hit on the truth. God's servant does not only have to speak and to act (and in speaking to act), he also has to suffer. Jeremiah was the martyr prophet, the prototype of Jesus, the man who not only sees and describes the action of God in judgement and mercy out in the world of striving men and women, but feels it, suffers it, and endures it in his own person.

Application

At the end of the day then, Jesus of Nazareth does not save us from the outcome of our endemic waywardness and foolishness by his words, be they ever so 'powerful before God and the whole people', but by his death and resurrection. There at Calvary he does not speak for us, he dies for us, having offered the perfect sacrifice of obedience to what is true, lovely, upright and of good report, in a way of which we are simply not capable. So he becomes our Saviour. We take him as such, we accept him, we rely on him, we rest ourselves in him, that is, put our faith in him. The two travellers came to understand this and, we may be sure, to act upon it, because further down the road as they walked along, the risen Christ himself joined them and explained it all. And when they reached Emmaus they had communion together. So they were 'in him' as St Paul would say, and this made them safe against anything that could possibly destroy them. What an Easter it was for them, but ours could be a parallel.

19 INTRODUCING MEN TO THE TRINITY

Matthew 28.19 (NEB) *'Baptize men everywhere in the name of the Father and the Son and the Holy Spirit'*

Here is a young man, a Communist, well-informed, ardent, disciplined, one of the most promising of his group, being instructed how he is to conduct himself in the industry where he has just been signed on for employment. 'I want you, wherever you go, and among whatever people you find yourself, to seize every opportunity to introduce them to the Marxist interpretation of life. It is what you believe and what you are confident will be for their benefit if they believe it too.'

We begin with this illustration in order to deal with the word 'baptize' in the text, because if we do not deal with it, it is likely to cause a deaf ear to be turned in its direction. Baptism is a 'churchy' word, an ecclesiastical word. But suppose the analogy be accepted, then here is the young Christ, well-informed, ardent and disciplined, addressing himself to his disciples gathered round him. 'I want you, wherever you go, and among whatever people you find yourselves, to seize every opportunity *to introduce them* to belief in the Father, the Son and the Holy Spirit. It is what you believe in yourselves and what you are confident will be for their benefit if they believe it too.'

And we are astonished! What difference can such a belief possibly make to people if they are introduced to it? What good can it possibly do to a bus driver, a refrigerator salesman, a dressmaker, or the manager of a laundry, to be introduced to the Father, the Son and the Holy Spirit? 'All the difference in the world' will be the honest answer of those who have experienced it for themselves. It alters a person's complete outlook on life, providing a purpose almost wholly lacking before. But not immediately. Do not let us deceive ourselves. It is no easy stance to come to the point of making. There are formidable difficulties to be overcome.

1 *God the Father*

Take first the belief in God the Father. Is the Divine Father-hood in any way obvious? That is to say, does God's care of people stand out a mile? Because that is what Fatherhood means in this connotation. What man would come to this conclusion if he were born on the pavements in Calcutta, and saw no prospect of living or of dying anywhere better than the pavements of Calcutta! Nor is there need to travel to Calcutta to encounter this problem. Children are born in every country of the world deformed, crooked and diseased, with no hope of a full life. If anyone has not encountered the sharp point of this aspect of human existence he should read Archie Hill's *Love Within Closed Walls*. It concerns a spastic child who lived till he was twenty-seven and then developed cancer. For all the long twenty-seven years he was unable to hear, speak, turn his head or perform his natural functions without help—almost a thing. Where does God come in all this? Or for that matter in a world in which there is the tsetse fly, the hookworm, bacteria and rabies? Whatever then we may say about belief in God the Father, it certainly is not trite, sickly or sentimental. Indeed, the first words of the Apostles' Creed are almost a broadside on experience. 'I believe in God the Father Almighty, maker of heaven and earth.' Well might we ask how any observant person could have got himself to the place of writing this down. Take up the newspaper any day, there is no edition without the report of some calamity somewhere. And the situation is not as one little girl posed the question at one of the BBC's popular 'Any Questions' sessions—'Why do not the newspapers report happy events?' The truth is, the ugly ones are more newsworthy, because they actually exist. 'O God', we feel the urge to cry out, if we are sensitive at all to others' pain, 'Why did you make a world like this?'

But at the end of the day when we have quietened down from our resentment, shouting and rebellion, we know in our bones that if we do not hold to the belief in God as Father against all odds—yes, even in the face of that man who found it in his heart to catch a young woman's back in the sights of his rifle just outside Belfast and pull the trigger, while she was pregnant and just out walking with her father—if we do not believe in 'God the Father Almighty, maker of heaven and earth', we are lost, we have no anchor at all, everything is futile, or in the sentiments of Jean Paul Sartre, 'life is absurd'.

Therefore we introduce men to belief in God the Father because without it the blackness is impenetrable. This belief provides a light by which to go on hoping, and while there is hope there is life.

2 *Jesus Christ his only Son our Lord*

Secondly, we introduce people to belief in the Son, that is, Jesus Christ. This belief is sharp and clear. It implies that what we know of the character and purpose of God is spread out before us as if it were on a table. Jesus was a man. He breathed as we breathe. His heart beat at a rate a cardiograph would register. His blood belonged to a distinctive blood group. He had to eat, drink, wash, clean his teeth, brush his hair and perform bodily functions. And the measure of our shock when we so describe him is the index of how hesitant we are to recognise him as a man. But such he was. The Apostles' Creed affirms that he suffered, died and was buried, as a man. That is to say he went through the range of experiences common to man, boyhood, youth, manhood. And then pain in the most cruel form of execution invented. All that life is spread out as it were on a table for us to examine. Why? Because in that life, in that death and in that resurrection, what God is and what God does is exhibited.

There is of course an exhibition of God in nature, in poetry, in music, and in science too, but it is fragmentary. The face of Jesus Christ is where we must look to see God as he really is, a God who not only creates but cares, and not only makes, but remakes. This is why we introduce men and women everywhere to 'the Son', so that they shall come to know what is the heart of the Father. Like Father, like Son, like Son, like

Father, or in the words of a striking text, 'No one has ever seen God; but God's only Son, he who is nearest to the Father's heart, he has made him known' (John 1.18 NEB).

3 The Holy Spirit

Thirdly, we introduce men everywhere to the Holy Spirit. Suppose we refrained from this. Suppose we stopped short at the Father and the Son. What difference would this abbreviation make? It would lead to fossilization of the gospel! If we did not include the Holy Spirit, we should have to say, 'Yes, maybe God created the world and sustains it. Yes, Jesus was the finest type of manhood known, pity we did not live in Palestine two thousand years ago, we might have encountered him ourselves.' But because we believe in the Holy Spirit we know that God operates in the lives of people *now*, lifting them up and often transforming their potentialities with unexpected results.

Here, for example, are three young men and two young women in a college at Oxford, all five of them from non-church-going homes whose lives have been so altered by responding to the Christian gospel that they have nothing to do with the promiscuity, rebellion and experimentation with drugs so common in their age group, but who are discovering instead ways of serving the community. Because of the Holy Spirit Christianity is not a museum exhibit, but a contemporary dynamic force actually changing the direction of people's lives with constructive results in place of drift. We introduce people therefore to the Father, the Son *and the Holy Spirit*, the one whom the Nicene Creed describes as 'the Lord and Giver of life'.

And now we must come back to that word 'baptize' in our text. 'Baptize men everywhere in the name of the Father and the Son and the Holy Spirit.' We substituted the word 'introduce' for 'baptize' as a means of gaining a hearing. But we cannot be satisfied with the substitute. We cannot let it stand. Those who are introduced to the faith and come to commit themselves to it mark their entry with a rite. It is carried out with water and the name of the Trinity. This is baptism, a sacrament, and a sacrament is not merely an indicator, it is a means of grace, an instrument by which strength comes from God to the one who receives it. So we not only introduce men everywhere to the name of the Father, the Son and the Holy Spirit, we baptize them *into the name*, so that by this sacrament they receive not only a new status but a new energy from that entry and from that status.

Here then we encounter the foundation on which the Church is built and so long as it is true to that foundation it will not fail. Indeed Christ added his own promise to his conviction, 'Go forth,' he said, ... 'make disciples ... baptise ... teach .... And be assured, I am with you always, to the end of time.'

20 THE INCLUSIVE CHRIST

Acts 4.12 (NEB) *'There is no salvation in anyone else at all, for there is no other name under heaven granted to men, by which we may receive salvation'*

That settles it! At least for some these words are absolutely final. 'There is no salvation in any one else at all.' So this current preoccupation with dialogue with men of faiths other than the Christian is not only waste of time, it is positively harmful, being unscriptural—'There is no other name under heaven'—What could be more clear or more decisive? Muslims, Buddhists, Hindus, yes, and even Jews, are all on the road that leads to perdition, and to have dealings with them on religious grounds as if this were not so is to deceive both them and ourselves. The name of Christ is the only name by which we may receive salvation.

1 *Exclusiveness*

If, however, some find this exclusive attitude satisfactory, even comforting, others are repelled by it. They hear this uncompromising rigidity on the part of St Peter standing in the dock in Jerusalem with dismay. He had been charged with healing a lame man in the name of Jesus. But he was not overawed by his captors as well he might have been, because the disparity between their social standing, their education, their general style and manner and his was wide and deep. But he displayed a boldness arresting even to that board of critics. And of course, they were in an awkward position. The cripple whom everyone entering the Temple by the gate called 'Beautiful' knew, because he had begged alms from his daily stance for so long, was now walking and praising God, the latter activity no less remarkable than the former. So they had to suffer Peter's boldness. He held the trump card. And they, Jews, had to suffer Peter's apparently exclusive assertion that there is 'no other name under heaven granted to men by which we may receive salvation'. Jews had to hear this. It is not difficult to estimate their reaction.

But the Jews also were exclusive. At least exclusiveness was the way Judaism had developed. It is true that teaching with the opposite attitude was explicit in their sacred writings, but this was not what found expression in later practice, and certainly not under the influence of the Pharisees in the time of Jesus and his disciples. Here then in the Jerusalem courtroom, on account of a cured cripple, two religions were facing each other with an apparently rigid exclusiveness—Judaism which had little room for the Gentiles, and embryonic Christianity in the person of Peter, spokesman for the twelve apostles which apparently had no room for any saviour other than the Saviour, Jesus.

So we arrive at an impasse. One group asserting—outside Judaism, no salvation! The other group asserting—outside Christ, no salvation! They could not both be right, and the logic seems obvious that they must both be wrong. And the answer on the lips of many will be: either all religions are delusions, or all religions are equally valid, which, in popular speaking, comes out as follows, 'We all worship the same God, are there not many roads to the same home?'

At this point it is necessary to pause and think deeply. We have to ask ourselves if the new preaching about Christ which is embodied in the New Testament really is exclusive. Let it be granted that Peter, in the early stage of his discipleship, fresh from the ranks of Judaism and to some extent still in those ranks, did think of Christ exclusively. He had yet to come face to face with a contradiction of seeing a Gentile receive the gift of God's Spirit in the same way as he, a Jew, had experienced him, and to have his mind broadened. But the facts are that the full New Testament new preaching does not proclaim Christ as exclusive but as *inclusive*. There is no other name by which men may receive salvation *for the very profound reason* that all salvation for everyone under whatever name it may have been received actually derives from Christ who is 'before all and through all and in all'.

Let an illustration assist. Here is a family, each member of which is engrossed in some different occupation in a different room in a house. Father is busy in the garage fixing the leads of his battery charger because he must give a boost to his car battery or he will never get the vehicle started in the morning, and his job, in a way his whole life, depends on his ability to use that car. It is his salvation. And mother in the kitchen has fixed up her ironing board because the whole family depends on her for clean clothes, washed, ironed and folded. John, aged twelve, upstairs, his bedroom decorated according to his taste, if not anyone else's, with garish posters, is absorbed with a new Black and Decker power drill he has been given. It makes a fearful noise, but his skill with that tool may be the means of earning him a livelihood before a few years are out. And Mary, aged ten, in the sitting room is lying on the floor watching a television programme absorbing her attention. Now comes the question. Which of those instruments filling out the lives of those four different people (if 'saving' them is too strong a word to use) is indispensable? Can it be asserted of any one of them that it only has a right to exist? Does not each one make the life of the person using it? So in a way it is their saviour. But think a little deeper. How is it that the battery charger works? And the iron, and the Black and Decker drill, and the television? Is it not because of the electricity that is available empowering all four tools for all four people? Is not then the real 'saviour' electricity, or even Michael Faraday who invented it, or he and they who developed it? So as far as that household is concerned it might be said in nothing else is there satisfaction or fulfilment for them but in electricity, it is *the inclusive* means by which each carries out his or her essential occupation.

In some such way as this the New Testament preaches its new gospel of Christ. There is no other name by which men may receive salvation because under whatever name it may have been received it actually derives from Christ of whom Paul wrote in the Epistle to the Colossians 1.17 (NEB), 'He exists before everything, and all things are held together in him.' Our text therefore does not present an exclusive proclamation of Christ after all, but *an inclusive*.

3 *Three conclusions*

If then this is the truth, if this really is what the New Testament preaches, certain conclusions follow.

First, we must not sweep away the lights by which others live, as if they were worthless, providing no light at all. This is not true. Granted the light may be feeble, flickering and in danger of extinction, but it is a serious matter to knock out of a person's hand whatever is the light by which he lives, for by so doing we may consign him to disaster. Jesus himself expressed this truth in strong terms in his story of the peril of an empty house where evils rush in and fill up the void, making the last state worse than the first. On the surface reckoning to divest whole races of their imperfect religion (and all religions are imperfect) may seem like deliverance, but if in its place there is given Western nihilism, secularism and godlessness, where is the advantage? The dispossessed know the answer— the last state is worse than the first.

Secondly, we must listen with respect to the testimonies which men of other faiths give to what their religion has done for them. We must also be ready to testify in their presence to what our faith has done for us. We must listen humbly and we must testify humbly. We must not claim to know the whole truth, even though we believe Christ to be the whole truth, for we shall recognise that we ourselves only know 'in part' and can only prophesy 'in part'. And if we find ourselves in dialogue with people of the Jewish faith, we shall tread even more delicately, conscious of the Church's shocking record in its dealings with this race of people. But if in this fashion we encounter men of other faiths, we shall see the light that shines for them enabling them to walk life's rough places common to us all, albeit with failures. And we shall expect that they for their part will see the light by which we live. We may hope and pray that they will turn to it, but if they do it will only be because they recognise the light of which they know something already in their own faith. So they will be turning to the One true light of which there are, and always have been since the world began, many reflections.

Thirdly, by looking sympathetically at other faiths by which men live, we shall arrive at a deeper awareness of our own. There are those who assert that in schools the only proper course is to teach all the religions. This is a pedagogic nonsense. The only successful approach is to be committed to one religion, and from this position of understanding to reach out sympathetically to the others and in the process to learn more deeply of the one.

And when the Christian does look out on other faiths is there any uniqueness for him to discover *in his own*? Yes, there is, and not least in the new proclamation about Jesus recorded in the fourth gospel, 'Who sees me sees the Father'. Let Jacques-Albert Cuttat, sometime Swiss diplomat and now Professor of Theology, express it in his own words. 'This is the completely new and unique feature of Christianity, namely, that the objective presence of a fully human being is the key of the door to that which is fully divine.' He goes on,

'In none of the Extra Christian traditions . . . do spiritual ways and divine truth coincide in the person of a historical man. The Buddha and the Hindu Guru . . . indicate to follow the mystic way; Christ is *the* way. The prophets of monotheistic religion receive and proclaim the revealed truth. Christ *is* the truth . . . The metaphysical East exalts knowledge as a means of spiritual development. Judaism and Islam emphasise faith as an instrument of salvation . . . The characteristic of Christianity is to unite these two elements without merging them into a single spiritual act . . . penetrating to the very heart of the divine perspective through the mediacy of human perspective. This characteristic has no equivalent outside Christianity . . . God is that which Christ reveals.'*

To put the matter in a nutshell. We see God in man, in a man, and that man is Jesus of Nazareth—this is the unique feature of Christian preaching.

We return to the point where we began, to St Peter with uplifted head and straightened back, standing in the Jerusalem court-room defending his act of healing in the name of Jesus. He refused to be silenced. And so should we. We should not be silenced in our pluralistic society. We have something, we have someone, to declare. But let us understand who that someone is. Jesus of Nazareth, unique, not as the Buddha is undoubtedly unique, and Lao-tse, and Confucius and Zoroaster too, but *unique because he is inclusive*, because he is comprehensive, or as Peter confessed, not knowing then the full depth of what he was saying, 'There is no salvation in anyone else at all, for there is no other name under heaven granted to men, by which we may receive salvation.'

* Pages 70-71 'The Encounter of Religions—a Dialogue Between the West and the Orient'.

Hebrew 13.8 (NEB) *'Jesus Christ is the same yesterday, today, and for ever'*

1 *Changes*

People who live in London rub their eyes every now and then to realise what changes are taking place all around them in the city's architecture and skyline. To feel the full impact of these changes it is only necessary to walk to the centre of Waterloo Bridge early one Sunday morning, when the lightness of the traffic provides sufficient respite to take in the scene. Everywhere new buildings are obvious. Everywhere is glaring evidence that the old London has almost disappeared. And the same holds true for other big cities in Britain—Birmingham, Coventry, Sheffield—the changes are enormous.

And if we looked out on most English villages today with eyes for the changes that have taken place, we should be astonished. The churches might tell of the past, the inn and perhaps a few of the houses. But the hard roadway, the garage and the supermarket indicate a very diffrent kind of village from that which used to exist.

And what about the clothes people wore a hundred years ago? So much black, so many layers of clothing, so much thick material. And the pace of everything would surprise us. Apart from the railway, everything was measured by the speed of an horse. And no telephone and no radio. Time was needed to convey news from one place to another.

And suppose by some magic process people who died a hundred years ago could suddenly come back today! They wouldn't know whether to laugh or cry. Imagine a lady in black bombazine, bonnet and bustle picking up one of our glossy magazines! Imagine a man seeing and hearing a jet aircraft making height after leaving Gatwick for Entebbe in Africa! And what about the television in the corner of almost everybody's room?

When we look back to that world of a hundred years ago we are tempted to reckon it as a world of peace and straight-forwardness. But was it? There was much ignorance, illness and a weaker hold on life. Churchgoing was more general, reaching about 28 per cent of the population. Now it is less than 10 per cent. All the same, there was much hypocrisy, a great deal of mere conformity, and a terrible gap between Church and Chapel, and between Anglican and Roman Catholic.

And the news from Europe was not reassuring. France was staggering under the aftermath of the Franco-Prussian war, and Germany was forging the weapons for military domination with the huge indemnity France had to pay. Altogether, a hundred years ago life was much as it is now; full of hopes *and* full of fears, full of things improved and full of things grown worse. People loved and people hated. Cloud and sunshine, health and sickness, life and death, pleasure and pain. These are the basic facts of life, they only change the colour of their clothes. Life is much the same, yesterday, today, and for ever, only the externals alter.

2 *Perennial needs*

So the question arises. Is the Christian faith outmoded as some try to tell us it is? Can we assert that it belongs only to the past, only marginally to the present, and probably has no future at all? No, we cannot! *People* are the same. *Life* is basically the same, and their needs stand out as ever they did.

What are people's perennial needs?

First, someone in whom to believe. This is half our trouble today. No one believes in anything or in anybody any more. We are suspicious of top people, suspicious of bottom people; we are suspicious of capital, suspicious of labour, suspicious of governments, politicians, big business, and the news media. We reckon we are being conned, cheated and 'led up the garden path.' The trouble with Britain today is that we no longer believe, no longer trust, no longer even profess a faith;

and when this situation is reached, the quality of life drops, even money is of less value.

What do people need?

Secondly, they need a basis for living. We all need it. We need a foothold, or to alter the metaphor, we need some boarding or planking across the swamps of life on which to set our feet. In the last two or three decades there have been too many changes; this is true even of Church life. Sometimes it appears as if we are making changes for change's sake. And the surprising result is a boring sameness. Go where you will in the world today, to London, to Leicester, to Los Angeles or Kwala Lumpur, you will find the same dreary high rise blocks of flats, the same concrete, the same square windows, the same skyline, the same sameness. But changes are only acceptable if we have a firm foundation under our feet, if we have solid answers to *basic* questions. Is there a God in heaven who cares? What is the purpose of my life? Is there a destiny for each one of us beyond the grave? Without basic answers to basic questions we lose our way among the changes and chances of this mortal life. We need to know where we stand as much as our grandparents did a hundred years ago.

What do people need?

They need a new sense of the worth of each individual. If industrialisation a hundred years ago turned people into 'hands', our contemporary electronic revolution has turned us into mere numbers on holes punched in a card for use in a computor. And if the present process of automation in factories and offices is enlarged, we shall become a nation of button-pushing operators of which the girl sitting at the cash desk in the supermarket is a prototype. Most alarming of all, most sinister of all, is the conditioning of individuals that goes on, not least by means of television, thinking the thoughts for us that we ought to think, selecting the clothes that we must wear, and even the processed foods we must eat tomorrow. So individualism is fast being ironed out, and our modern unrest and occasional rebellion is the sign of modern man's protest.

3 Unchanging Christ

Here then the Church stands offering the modern world some-one in whom to believe and whom to trust: 'Jesus Christ is the same yesterday, today, and for ever.' Here is the foundation on which to set our feet in an age of frequent change. 'Jesus Christ is the same yesterday, today, and for ever.' Here is a gospel which, while it accepts the importance of society, sets a high price on the worth of every individual. The Church indeed is only justifying its existence in so far as it is offering the contemporary world this everlasting gospel of salvation. Every age needs it. The Victorian age with its sentimentality, prudery, and hypocrisy, yes, and goodness as well as sins. But thank God, every age has the good news of salvation ready to hand, for 'Jesus Christ is the same yesterday, today, and for ever'.

Away then with our inferiority complex. Away with the agonizing over the Church's rôle in contemporary society. Let every member of every congregation thank God for what has been given him in the message of Christ crucified and risen—'the same yesterday, today, and for ever.' The Church still has, and always will have, an essential rôle—it is to cele-brate the gospel, to proclaim the gospel, and to live the gospel. If it does this, of one thing it can be certain—it will never be outmoded.

Acts 11.17 (NEB) 'God gave them no less a gift than he gave us when we put our trust in the Lord Jesus Christ'

I do not suppose Cornelius sported a 'handle-bar' moustache but he might have done had he been encountered at Sandhurst in 1977 because the army was his métier. He was, in fact, a captain, or more exactly a centurion in the Italian Cohort drafted for service in Palestine and based on Caesarea, the garrison town where Pontius Pilate, the Roman Governor, had his headquarters. He could scarcely have been true to type. Romans in general displayed few religious inclinations beyond what were serviceable for the State. They were realistic administrators whose ascendency in the world depended to no small extent on the disciplined efficiency of their armies. The rank and file of the troops would be tough, brutal and coarse, not least in Palestine where religious taboos inflamed either their mockery, their resentment or both. How comes it then, that of Cornelius we read, 'He was a religious man, and he and his whole family joined in the worship of God. He gave generously to help the Jewish people, ar ¹ was regular in his prayers to God.' We do not know the answer to this question, but it is a salutary reminder not to write off any man because of his profession.

Cornelius, however, is significant for a deeper reason. His story is recounted at some length in the book of the Acts of the Apostles because the spiritual experience that came to him marks a turning point in the history of the Christian Church. Cornelius was a 'Goy'. Religious he might be, and charitable towards Israel, but neither of these praiseworthy characteristics changed the blood that ran in his veins, it was 'outsider's' blood, non-Jewish blood. Cornelius, in short, was a Gentile, a 'Goy,' a man, therefore, on an altogether different plane when it came to his standing before God. The infant Christian Church, cradled in Judaism, held firmly to this Jewish conviction, although badly shaken, first by Samaritans responding to the gospel of Christ and then by the conversion of an Ethiopian, a high official of the Kandake, doubtless a coloured man. But Cornelius' case was even more questionable. He stood for all the great powers who down through history had suppressed God's chosen people, Syria, Assyria, Babylon and now Rome. True individuals among these nations might benefit from the *uncovenanted* mercies of God, but they could never be on a par with the elect nation. It is over against this conviction that the comment on Cornelius' experience, and that of his family, made by no less a person than Peter himself, and the members of the Church *in Jerusalem*, stands out like a neon sign. 'God gave them no less a gift than he gave us when we put our trust in the Lord Jesus Christ.'

Racial equality

Now that this milestone in Church history has been passed, however, what has the Cornelius event to say to us? Three principles at least. First, that race does not disqualify in the matter of a man's standing before God. 'I now see' said Peter to Cornelius, his relatives and his close friends, 'how true it is that God has no favourites, but that in every nation the man who is god-fearing and does what is right is acceptable to him.' This seems clear enough. In 1977 we take it lying down. Suppression of black minorities, and worse still, black majorities, is generally, though not universally unacceptable today. We believe in human rights. But, laudable as this is, it is not what this scripture is about, though it may well be traceable to it. The Cornelius story is about human privileges, not about human rights. We have *no rights* before God. Nor can we ever build up any rights or claims upon God. Jesus made this startlingly plain with his story of the labourers in the vineyard. Each set of men, whether hired at the beginning of the day or towards sunset, received the same pay regardless of hours. And when those who had toiled through 'the burden and heat of the day' complained, reckoning that they had surely built up rights or claims upon their employer, they scarcely received a hearing. So the whole concept of man's acquiring merit before God is demolished. We have no rights. Ah! but we have privileges! And this is what the Cornelius story is about. To every man, woman and child, no matter what racial blood trickles through his veins, no matter what the colour of his skin, nor even the state of his health, physical or even moral (this is the marvel), God offers, yes offers, the privilege of being called his son. Even more, every man is God's elect, if only he will accept the election. What could be more open and generous! And this act of grace, be it noted, basic in the God-man relationship, preserves the rights of man vis-à-vis *other men* from running into a dangerous stridency, leading even to bloodshed, as appears to happen all too frequently when the drift away from Christian origins becomes secularized. Every man has his rights but he has them as a gift from God. Forget this and the struggle for human rights is fraught with danger.

2 *The conversion of a good man*

A second observation to make from this story is that goodness is not enough. Is this surprising? When however the account of Cornelius in the book of the Acts of the Apostles informs us that 'he was a religious man, and he and his whole family joined in the worship of God. He gave generously to help the Jewish people, and was regular in his prayers to God'. When we read this, need we be surprised if the question arises, wherein then lay the need for anything further? Have we not here an exemplary figure? And the inquiry takes to itself some urgency in the 1970s when the discovery is being made, not least by Christians, that religions other than Christianity have truth in them as well. What then did Cornelius lack? And the answer is Christ. He had heard *about* Christ, as is evident from Peter's address to him and his friends, but he had not committed himself *to* Christ, but when he did so he entered into a new experience which transcends all that he had known before. Bonhoeffer would say it marked for Cornelius the end of religion and the beginning of life 'in Christ'. No longer was he striving to reach God, albeit with commendable zeal; from now on he was allowing God to reach him by means of Christ with all the resources of his grace and power. Cornelius was like an architect striving to erect a bridge by which to cross a deep and wide chasm to reach a better life on the opposite bank, only to have pointed out to him that further down stream, where the chasm was at its widest and deepest, a bridge had already been erected from the opposite bank to his bank and nothing remained but for him to cross it. That bridge is Christ. The story of Cornelius then is the story of *a good man* being converted to Christ crying aloud the New Testament preaching, not that religion, prayers and almsgiving outside Christ are worthless, on the contrary, these make the doer acceptable to God whatever his nationality—but that the fullness of God's gift available to all has not been enjoyed until Christ has been recognised and trusted. Christianity, when it is true to the New Testament, does not denigrate all other religions by saying, 'Look, you are all wrong and we are all right.' It says, 'We have found, and you, too, will find, a richness in Christ, surpassing all the efforts either of us could ever muster.'

3 Baptism in the Spirit

It is remarkable how contemporary the Cornelius story is. It gives light on at least three points of modern inquiry. First, about the rights of man. Secondly, about the relation of Christianity to other faiths, and thirdly, about the charismatic movement. It is to this last that we now turn.

When Cornelius, his relatives and his close friends expectantly (very important, this) listened to Peter preaching Christ to them in his house at Caesarea—what a setting it was for the preacher! Being a Jew, he had never even seen inside a Gentile room before—fresh spiritual life burst into being which the book of the Acts of the Apostles describes as the outpouring of the Holy Spirit. The congregation that day began 'to speak with tongues of ecstasy and acclaiming the greatness of God'. Here all at once there was a live Church in a man's house. It was as if the paper and sticks were laid ready and prepared in the fireplace, ready to burst into flame as soon as they were touched by the match of Peter's proclamation of Christ.

Is this outburst of new spiritual life what should always take place at the moment of commitment to Christ? Does the outpouring of the Spirit take place at conversion? Are we to associate the descent of the Spirit with the sacramental expression of this initial experience in baptism? This is a matter the theologians, both within and without the modern charismatic movement are discussing. Some take this Cornelius story as the norm. Others (mistakenly in my judgement) take it as abnormal and look for a double Christian experience, asserting that first there comes conversion and water baptism making second-class Christians, and later for a special few there comes baptism in the Spirit, making for first-class Christians. Both schools of thought must, however, agree in this, that it is the Spirit who gives life, irrespective of race, or as Peter put it at Jerusalem, 'God gave them no less a gift than he gives us when we put our trust in the Lord Jesus Christ; then how could I possibly stand in God's way?'

None of us ought ever to stand in God's way. That to do so is possible speaks volumes about the nature of God's sovereignty, and the reality of the freedom granted to man. We ought not to deny to all men everywhere for reasons of snobbery or economic gain the gifts of God which are available for ourselves. We ought not to close our own hearts to the love of God which he has brought to us in Christ. We ought not to stand in God's way of bringing about a charismatic renewal in our day by the outpouring of his Spirit. This is the lesson. Be open to God's leading as Peter was open to it, obeying the promptings which urged him to cross the threshold of a Roman army captain to proclaim Christ to him. When those ten men including Peter took the coast road that day from Simon the tanner's house in Joppa to Cornelius' house in Caesarea, they made history. History could be made for us if we likewise determine to be open to Christ, open to his Spirit and open to people, as God himself is open to us.

23 THE NOON-DAY

Acts 26.3 (NEB) *'Your Majesty, in the middle of the day I saw a light from the sky, more brilliant than the sun . . .'*

Introduction

When the exterior of St Paul's Cathedral was cleaned some years ago, features of the stonework stood out in a way they had not done for years. One was the representation of the conversion of St Paul carved high up under the apex of the West Front, presenting, so to speak, the message of the building to all who approach it. This was noted by *The Times* with a photograph reproduced in one of its editions. It is to this incident that our text refers.

1 *St Paul's noonday experience*

Now there came a day in the life of this man when he had occasion for the second time to describe the incident in his own words. It took place in the presence of King Agrippa and Queen Berenice at Caesarea, and this is what he said, 'Your Majesty, in the middle of the day I saw a light from the sky, more brilliant than the sun . . . '

It is to this observation of a light more brilliant than the *noonday* sun that we give our attention. In Psalm 91 we read of the plague or sickness that destroys at the *noonday*. Here from Paul's lips we hear of a light breaking in to remake a man *at the noonday*!

Would it be fanciful to suggest that Saul of Tarsus at the time of this incident had reached *the noonday* of his career and it was destroying him? He was at the height of his natural powers and they were considerable. He had 'arrived' so to speak, in his world. He had letters from the High Priest at

Jerusalem authorizing him to root out adherents of the new sect at Damascus. Educated, experienced, equipped and energetic—Saul of Tarsus was confident of himself (or so it appeared). He was a man on the promotion list.

2 Noondays in life

Would it also be fanciful to suggest that there is a plague or sickness liable to destroy any one of us of all ages, at the noonday of our lives?

Here is a married couple. They have shared each others' lives for fifteen years. Neither of them contemplates breaking up the marriage, but they simply take each other for granted. They do not have rows. They are simply bored with each other. That is the danger, the sickness that destroys at the noonday.

Here is a professional man aged about forty. Of him it could be stated that he had 'made the grade'. His skills are recognized. He has become a man reckoned worth while to consult. But fresh ideas no longer well up in his mind. The moment he quits his desk at 5.30 p.m. he closes his mind entirely on his work. See him and the evidence of a growing laziness will be obvious. He has settled down. Do not expect much of that man in five years' time. The sickness that destroys at the noonday has taken hold of him, leading to mediocrity, if not something worse.

Here is a church, here is a clergyman, here is a professing Christian, man or woman, who have lived for years by the light of the gospel. If the truth were known, quite a number of people encountering them in the past have had their lives lifted on to another level on account of the witness they have given by deed and by word. But not now. They do not reach out any more. They have turned in on themselves, grumbling about the state of the world, the Church, the new forms of worship, the ecumenical movement, and, or at worst, their own illnesses. This is the sickness that destroys at the noonday, making their faith a debilitated thing.

Here is the British nation at the present time, with its long history of industrial achievement, and a record for assistance in many good causes throughout the world, albeit with self-interest in the mixture of motives. But what has happened to us? We go cap-in-hand to the International Monetary Fund, to the European Economic Corporation, to Germany, to the U.S.A., anyone who will lend us money. Where is our pride, our confidence, our faith? Can this be another case of the sickness that destroys at the noonday?

3 *Brighter than the noonday*

And now we turn back to the text, 'Your Majesty, at the middle of the day I saw a light from the sky, more brilliant than the sun.'

Religion, the Church's religion, is not simply morality touched with emotion. It is not merely a set of rules of behaviour, hemming us in to a life of negatives. Nor is Christianity ecclesiastical organisation, synods, conferences, councils and schemes for raising money. Nor is it anyone's pathetic attempts to pull himself up by his own bootlaces. The Christian gospel tells of a *power outside* which breaks into people's lives, a power they do not conjure up themselves, or even think up themselves. If then there is a sickness that destroys at the noonday, there is also an outside power which can give health at the noonday. 'Your Majesty, in the middle of the day I saw a light from the sky, more brilliant than the sun.' This is the importance of keeping alive the memory of Paul's conversion on the Damascus road. There is a power of God able to lift us out of the boredoms, the depressions, the sluggishness and the mediocrity into which we so easily slip when we are successful or merely take life for granted. We need power of another dimension and any Christian proclamation or fellowship which does not reckon *with this* has succumbed to the sickness which destroys at the noonday.

And someone wishes to object. 'All this is only traditional Christianity, Christianity according to the book, Christianity as it was in the days of Paul, but not now!' Listen! Here is a city clerk, not even baptised, but he happened to read a book. Now he is an ordained minister. How do you explain it? Here is a man in prison, angry and bitter with society, now he is the most helpful Christian in that strange gaoled community. How do you explain it? Here is a woman, a factory worker, whose marriage has broken, but who has found new life and happiness through the ministrations of a curate at the local parish church to which she was almost a stranger. How do you explain it?

Is not this contemporary evidence of authentic Christianity? God's power breaking in to remake, renew and equip?

Application

Tomorrow you will take up your daily work again, and so shall I. Have I to solve all those problems myself? Have you to solve yours? These are questions to which we do not know the answers. There are stretches ahead of us on the road which are shrouded in darkness. There are blind corners and dangerous bends. Christianity is no more use to us than extra baggage if it does not only tell us, but also introduces us to the light that will enable us to do what is otherwise impossible.

'Your Majesty, in the middle of the day I saw a light from the sky, more brilliant than the sun . . . ' and I was not disobedient to the heavenly vision.

24 THE OUTWARD AND INWARD MAN

2 Corinthians 4.16 (RV) ' . . . *though our outward man is decaying, yet our inward man is renewed day by day*'

'Look younger, live longer.' This was the title of the one book that could be seen through the window of the smart house in the London square with its 'good address', where a young couple had taken up residence. Clearly life for them was 'a good thing', and they were 'on the make'. They intended squeezing every drop of pleasure possible from the fruits of their own energies and the good fortune that had befallen them. Any suggestion that they, like everybody else, were on the way to die as soon as they were born, would have been scornfully rejected as morbid. They were typical of twentieth-century man and woman who, flushed with the rewards of contemporary technology, have turned their backs, not only on death, but on the failing powers that precede it. 'Look younger, live longer.' This is the up-to-date slogan.

But is this wise? The story is told of a French Marquise who received an invitation to a dinner party he could not attend, and for this reason, that he was on his death-bed when the message arrived. 'Tell my charming hostess,' he replied, 'that I much regret I am unable to accept because, unfortunately, I have to die.' Not perhaps an altogether bad reason for others of us absenting ourselves from pleasures apparently less innocuous than a dinner party. We all have to die.

But why worry? Is not death indispensable? Where would be the living space for a growing population if death did not daily provide the gaps the rising generation requires? Dead men's shoes are after all a vital necessity. So while there is death there is hope, hope for a good life for our children coming on. Or stand back a little from life in its totality, death is a necessary step in the evolutionary process of nature. Teilhard de Chardin has described it as 'the essential lever in the mechanism and upsurge of life.' That which dies and decays today forms the compost which enriches the life of tomorrow.

Is not modern man on the right track then when he raises his telescope to his blind eye as far as the enemy called—or perhaps miscalled—death is concerned? Apparently not. That is to say, he is unable to manage the subterfuge and the reason is because death for man involves meaninglessness. Perhaps no-one has expressed this more vividly than Sartre when he says, 'Man is a useless passion. To get yourself drunk by yourself in a bar, or to be a leader of the nations is equally pointless.' And Bertrand Russell expressed the same in his biography when he told us that throughout his life he sought the ecstasy of sexual love because it relieves 'that terrible loneliness in which one shivering consciousness looks over the ruin of the world into the cold, unfathomable, lifeless abyss'.

St Paul, however, thought otherwise. Writing to the Christians of Corinth, he said, 'though our outward man is decaying, yet our inward man is renewed day by day.'

1 *The outward man*

First note how Paul was under no illusions about the increasing limitations of our physical capacities of which we become aware all too soon as we grow older . . . 'though our outward man is decaying . . . ' Not that the boxer still in his twenties would describe his condition in this way, but he knows that very soon now he will be too old for 'the ring', already he has reached his prime. Nor are they the words of a man unexpectedly made reflective because he has discovered that his son can run faster than he can. The passing of the years deals even more hardly on woman. Unless she is philosophical she will not reach the period when she can no longer bear a child without depression. Paul may not have understood how the cells in the body are constantly dying and regenerating with decreasing potentiality, but he knew how soon the time arrives when there is something we cannot manage this year which we could last year—'our outward man is decaying.'

2 *The inward man*

Before, however, Paul has finished his sentence, he supplies a compensating statement, 'our inward man is renewed day by day.' This also is true. Youth may be resilient, strong and free, but it is also restless, rebellious and irresponsible. When, however, youth passes, it gives way to a steadiness less exciting, no doubt, but opening up the possibility of citizenship, family life and the advancement of some skill or profession. And when in turn this middle-age period passes, there slips away some of its earthiness, materialism and stodginess which too often characterize it, giving birth in its place to reflection on the meaning of life for which the term wisdom is not wholly inappropriate—'though our outward man is decaying, our inward man is renewed day by day.'

3 *The reinforcing faith*

But even this is not the whole story. How could it be without plunging us into deeper pointlessness? Our outward man is decaying, our inward man is being renewed—but what for? What is the point of one phase giving way to another phase— or perhaps better 'giving birth'—if there is to be a last phase which gives way to nothingness? Does not the apparent progression from material to spirit mock us unmercifully if all is to end in a blank wall? And this of course is what Sartre and Bertrand Russell sensed so acutely. The facts are that experience presents us with two possibilities—or three if burying our heads in the sand is counted one—either meaninglessness or faith.

What is faith? Certainly not credulity. But is it wishful thinking? Yes, there is an element of wishful thinking in faith, but it does not therefore invalidate it. Our longings may indeed be rough indicators, not merely of what we invent, but of what exists. Faith is a leap beyond evidence but it is not a leap *without evidence*. It does not jump from nowhere to somewhere. It jumps from somewhere which has all the signs of being a stepping-stone to somewhere better.

See how this is true to experience. The young man's physical strength begins to fail, but it gives birth to a period of solid achievement. This in turn passes away and with it the poverty of middle-aged mediocrity, but it goes on to give birth to the wise old man whose strength is spirit. Notice the use of the word 'birth' here. If then all these 'little deaths' on the way to the final death carry with them a new birth to something deeper, more refined, more spiritual, is it unreasonable to suppose that the so-called final death is also a birthday to a life infinitely better, indeed, eternal life itself? From this plank of reasonableness then we make the jump of faith into the confession as summarised in the Apostles' Creed, 'I believe . . . in the resurrection of the body, and the life everlasting.'

But this is not all. We do not jump out into the dark to fumble our way unassisted. There approaches through the gloom a shining Presence even before we make our leap, lighting up the other side, it is the risen Christ. He comes to us from the pages of Scripture, from the worshipping assembly of his people, from the arresting goodness shown towards us by some man, some woman, whom we are driven in consequence to call a 'saint'. This risen Christ reinforces the feeling 'in our bones' that the outward decay we experience coupled with the inward renewal, points to something beyond the incidence of physical death, and we are prepared to believe therefore in the life eternal and to guide our lives thereby.

Dag Hammarskjöld wrote, 'In the last analysis it is our conception of death which decides our answers to all the questions that life points to us.' It could be wondered if anyone lived under greater pressure day by day than this former Secretary-General of the United Nations who lost his life while on duty. Let us then come to terms with death now and we shall be freed for life now. This is what Sir Francis Chichester did, and why he put to sea on his last voyage, well aware that he was suffering from an incurable illness. We may try to live without death, that is, shutting our eyes to its incidence, but this is the way of failure. It is also the modern fashion, 'Look younger—live longer.' Wisdom counsels us to 'live with death'. It leads neither to morbidity nor inactivity. Let Dag Hammarskjöld and Sir Francis Chichester be witnesses. Rather does it lead to realism and reality. And the Christian has the promise of eternal life to reinforce his resolve, and not only the promise, but the grace of God too, indeed though his outward man is decaying the eternal life is within him already through faith in the risen and ever present Christ.

25 VIGILANCE

Hebrews 12.15, 16 (RV) ' . . . looking carefully lest there be any man that falleth short of the grace of God; lest any root of bitterness springing up trouble you, and thereby the many be defiled; lest there be any fornicator, or profane person, as Esau, who for one mess of meat sold his own birthright'

The time arrived when wisdom indicated a move from a large house to a smaller. The reasons can be guessed. So the turning out process began, a painful undertaking. A start was made on the attic, and in particular with an old leather suitcase, appallingly heavy and full of old papers. Was there anything of value in it? Anyway, it must be examined. But the task stopped halfway. A letter (was it really a letter?), turned up with no address attached and no signature. Who on earth was the author? To whom was it written and why? There were no clues beyond the contents of the letter itself, indeed, the mind of Sherlock Holmes would be necessary even to ferret out possibilities.

We possess a letter in the New Testament similar to this— the Epistle to the Hebrews. As one of the early Church Fathers commented (not flippantly), 'Who wrote the Epistle to the Hebrews, God only knows.' But reading the letter itself we are able to deduce that those to whom it was written were growing sluggish in their Christian profession, and needed stiffening. They had their difficulties of course, but they were not all that serious. It was true they pulled themselves together. They should begin by asking themselves these questions: 'What spiritual progress has our community made? Has bitterness taken root among us? Are we lax as regards immorality and profanity?'

If you have not thrown your Authorized Version of the Bible away, or the Revised Version, and that would be a very silly thing to do, good and helpful as the New English Bible may be, you will see that in Chapter 12 v 15-16 of the letter, the words 'looking carefully' are followed by the word 'lest' three times—'looking carefully lest . . .' 'looking carefully lest . . .' 'looking carefully lest . . .'. And even beginners with the Greek Testament will be able to see how the structure of the original has been followed in the Authorized Version, making clear three possible sores that need watching, Stagnation, Bitterness, and Profanity.

1 *Stagnation*

How does a Church become stagnant? There is nothing very attractive about stagnant water; it can in fact be positively dangerous to health. No nation knows this better than the Dutch who see to it that the water in their canals is constantly being changed. And herein lies the secret. Even the possessor of the humblest goldfish pool in his suburban garden knows it. Stagnation occurs in default of change. And yet we hear of congregations requesting no change in their church life; what is more remarkable, rural congregations close up to the changing seasons as no urban one can ever be, urging this very same plea. But nothing remains the same in nature. Day and night, summer and winter, calm and storm—some of the changes regular, some quite irregular—call for perpetual adaptation. A Church therefore becomes stagnant if it refuses to adapt to the climate in which its life is set. This does not mean swift and sudden changes. Nature never operates in this fashion. On the contrary, gradualness is the norm. Nor is there change for change's sake. Nor complete change without a permanent underlying structure. But all living things, as opposed to dead things, perpetually react to external changes. There is not therefore one mode of worship proper for all times and in all places, not one style of church architecture no, not even Gothic, which must always be copied. To be unwilling for change is to deny the manifold grace of God, it is to miss out on opportunities, it is to fall short of the grace of God. The anonymous letter to the Hebrews warns us to look carefully lest this happens to us. A Church, an individual

Christian who refuses to adapt though of course still holding fast his Christian faith and conduct becomes like stagnant water, unattractive to behold and dangerous to use.

2 Bitterness

We are also to look carefully for roots of bitterness. The phrase conjures up pictures of the gardener looking carefully over his plot to see if there exists any trace of what the English call 'ground elder', and the Scots, 'bishop's weed' (and thereby hangs a tale), because once this weed gets a hold no end of trouble will ensue. It may become necessary to dig out the whole of the herbaceous border because this weed twines itself around the roots of any plant it comes near, strangling its development. So acts bitterness in the human heart. It is a killer of all joy, spontaneity and progress. And it must be uprooted at the first sign of its appearance, it really must, because that is what it is, a root which spreads under the ground. Therefore, husband, out with that grudge at once with your wife because she does not feel like giving you what you want when you want it. Wife, out with that resentment today, not tomorrow, because he arrived home too late to give you an evening's outing. Son, daughter, out with that sneaking intention to take it out on your parents for objecting to the company you have started to keep. Husband, wife, son, daughter, you may have a case, but if, because of it, you let bitterness get a hold of you, you have put paid not only to spontaneity and progress in your own life, but in that of the whole family circle as well . . . . 'Looking carefully lest any root of bitterness trouble you and thereby the many be defiled.'

Unfortunately, it is not only against members of the family that people develop grudges, but against their employers, other classes, other races, even against society as a whole, and worst of all, most pernicious of all and most stupid of all, against God. The choir-boy who refuses to attend church any more because he was asked to leave the choir when his voice broke. The woman who writes to the Archbishop telling him that she has become an agnostic because her divorced daughter could not be married in the local parish church. These roots of bitterness should be uprooted at once or they will spread. Christians must go over the ground of their lives to see that they are 'grudge free' people.

3 Profanity

'Looking carefully . . . lest there be any fornicator, or profane person, as Esau, who for one mess of meat (or as the NEB puts it, "for a single meal") sold his own birthright.' Do not miss the reference to Esau. His name has not been included merely for the sake of literary embroidery; on the contrary, it indicates the kind of fornicator or profane person who brings ruin if not uprooted. This is the man or woman who fornicates or is profane, because he has come to the point of taking a low view of his spiritual inheritance. This is the person who not only does not practise what he preaches any more, but actually preaches what he practises, which is worse. In any Christian congregation there are people who have committed, are committing, fornication, let us face it. It ought not to be, but it is. The Church is not yet 'without spot or wrinkle', as St Paul put it. Christians are still men and women of flesh and blood with hungers that sometimes become intolerable. Temptations arise. Falls are experienced. Sins are committed, and sins they are. And when Jesus said that to want to go to bed with a woman is tantamount to doing so, who is innocent? 'Let him that is without sin first cast a stone.' No, but Esau was not sorry for what he had done. There lies the difference. There are men and women who boast of fornication, propagate it, and trade in the things of the Spirit for it. The writer of this letter calls them profane. And this is arresting. Profanity is an attitude we might have referred exclusively to the divine. A profane person is a blasphemous person, So he is, but a profane person is also one who deliberately treats the body of someone of the opposite sex as an instrument for individual pleasure, regardless of consequence to that other person. This is blasphemy against the Spirit. It is profanity. And the terror of the situation is that clever people can put up arguments to loosen manners so that to slip into this grave of profanity engenders little resistance. We need to look carefully in all matters concerned with sex. In this area of life the Latin tag holds good— the corruption of the best in the world—*corruptio optimi pessima*. We must be on our guard and the first piece of ground to go over is not the life of the Church, nor that of our neighbours, but our own hearts, remembering that it is the pure in heart who see God, and that the purity exists in our case not on account of sinlessness, but of divine forgiveness and cleansing.

Who were these Christians to whom the Epistle to the Hebrews was written? They must have been of Hebrew origin because they were expected to respond to arguments in a large part of the letter which were shot through with major Old Testament themes. But does it matter that we do not know? Churches, individual Christians, not excluding ourselves, can be in like case with these first readers, stagnant, bitter and profane. The first step for improvements is not to deny the existence of weeds in the garden, but to go and uproot them and then turn to the forgiveness and grace of God to make us the kind of attractive people we really should be and can be.

26 A TRIUMPHANT FAITH

Thessalonians 4.16-18 (RV) '*For the Lord himself shall descend from heaven, with a shout, with the voice of the archangel, and with the trump of God: and the dead in Christ shall rise first: then we that are alive, that are left, shall together with them be caught up in the clouds, to meet the Lord in the air: and so shall we ever be with the Lord. Wherefore comfort one another with these words'*

I wonder if you've got problems? Most people have problems. Churches certainly have problems. But the Church in Thessalonica had an unusual problem. It concerned the members of their community who had died. But what worried them was not the ugly gap the loss of these friends meant for the fellowship, but the haunting fear that because they had died they would miss out on the great drama of the Lord's return in glory soon to take place. The situation is comparable to the case of a man upon whom a great honour had been conferred. People said, 'What a pity his mother has just died. She would have loved seeing her son attend at the Palace for an Investiture.'

And we rub our eyes. Were there people who actually believed in this fashion in the Lord's second coming? Believing it to be so imminent, that it would take place in their own life time? And what really troubled them was the fear that some of these friends who had died would miss the Lord's return in power and great glory, when 'every eye would see him, and they also which pierced him'.

What makes us rub our eyes even more is that Paul did not comfort them by saying, 'Never fear, the Lord's coming will not take place for a long time, indeed a great many more of you will have died before it happens.' Nor did he assert that no such event as the Lord's second coming would ever take place. What Paul did was to comfort the Thessalonian Church with the information that those who had died would not miss out in the great drama of the Lord's coming, because the dead would be raised first, and caught up to meet the Lord in the air, so they would be ever with the Lord; the Thessalonians should 'comfort one another with these words'.

1 *The apparent irrelevance*

It is doubtful if today many people will find comfort in these words, unless they happen to have been brought up in that strict evangelical sect called The Plymouth Brethren for whom details of the manner of the Lord's second coming form a plank of basic belief. But for us, surrounded as we are today with signs of economic disaster (if we do not change our national way of life) and hijacking, kidnapping, drug-smuggling, traffic-congested cities, abortion, euthanasia, scientific medicine which can and sometimes does unduly prolong life, hunger in the third world, the arms race, battered daily by incessant news bulletins about the latest of these worries, it is unlikely that many people will be on the wavelength of these Thessalonians worrying about the Lord's second coming, or even on Paul's wavelength answering them as he did. Indeed, the very fact that their expectations were not fulfilled, that the Lord's second coming did not take place in their life time nor in ours two thousand years later, makes us switch off the whole theme.

2 The Lord reigns

Yet there is something to be said on the subject. It is an invitation to note the astonishing sweep of these people's Christian faith. Not for them the idea that the Christian religion is a harmless idiosyncracy for those few people who happen to like it, or to be 'made that way', but having little connection with the great world of affairs. On the contrary, Christ is *the* King, *the* Lord, *the* One in whom the whole history of the world consists and will one day *be seen* to consist. The Christian gospel is not a sectional affair. It is the hinge upon which the whole cosmic process turns.

So this is what this subject cries aloud. Look around. Christ does not *at the moment* reign supreme. If anything seems to come closest to reigning supreme *at the moment*, it is inflation; but look a little more closely. Is it not true that *underlying* our economic troubles, our sociological troubles and our international troubles is a great moral vacuum? Is it not true that we have lost our way in matters of right and wrong, good and bad, truth and expediency, and are therefore floundering? Where are the great men? the men with principle, the men with ideals and a willingness to sacrifice for their sake? Are we not drifting down to littleness of stature, meanness and perpetual retreat? So today if we clean our spectacles we can see *in reverse* how Christ reigns, for when the principles for which he stands are neglected, a slow breakdown ensues. Not many people admit this truth, but one day it will be obvious for all to see. That moment of truth, that sudden awareness, that startling revelation of God, and not man, as the Lord of all life will be Christ's second coming. It is different from the Lord's coming in humility at Bethlehem, different from the Lord's coming into your heart and mine, different from his coming in Word and Sacrament; this coming will be a public recognition by the world, that spiritual factors in the last resort *are the controlling power of the world's life*, in other words, Christ's reign.

Does this change the thrust of Paul's words? It does not. These Thessalonians lived in an historical period when the Church was far more of a minority movement than it is in Britain today. It seemed almost completely irrelevant to the stirring events that were occurring in the Roman Empire, but still they believed that *Christ would triumph*. Paul believed it. He said, 'The Lord himself shall descend from heaven, with a shout, with the voice of the archangel, and with the trump of God.' Certainly he used symbolic language suitable to those first century ears—but he and the Thessalonians believed in the face of their own desperate situation that Christ would finally triumph—that is the remarkable fact.

3 *Appeal*

And what about our decade? What about the Christians in our locality? Have we not allowed the problems and diffi-culties of our times to swamp and depress us, almost some-times blotting out the buoyancy in our faith? This then is the call of this scripture, to allow God, by his grace, to rekindle in our hearts a strong faith in Christ's final triumph in the world, a time when men will see that what Christ stands for is the basic necessity for all successful living. We need to pray for the recovery of this buoyant faith:

> Christ has died,
> Christ is risen,
> Christ will come again,

because this faith is what makes for triumphal, energetic and joyful living, the hall mark of being a Christian—'even so, come, Lord Jesus!'